The Longest Game

The Longest Game
Winning in Life

ADAM BURT

Carpenter's Son Publishing

The Longest Game: Winning in Life
Copyright ©2025 Adam Burt

All rights reserved. No part of this book may be reproduced or transmitted in any form or by any means, electronic or mechanical, including photocopying, recording, or by any information storage and retrieval system, without permission in writing from the copyright owner.

Scripture quotations marked (ESV) are from the ESV® Bible (The Holy Bible, English Standard Version®), copyright © 2001 by Crossway, a publishing ministry of Good News Publishers. Used by permission. All rights reserved.

The Holy Bible, Berean Study Bible, BSB, Copyright ©2016, 2018 by Bible Hub. Used by Permission. All Rights Reserved Worldwide.

Scripture quotations marked (NIV) are taken from the Holy Bible, New International Version®, NIV®. Copyright © 1973, 1978, 1984, 2011 by Biblica, Inc.™ Used by permission of Zondervan. All rights reserved worldwide. www.zondervan.com

Holy Bible, New Living Translation (NLT), copyright © 1996, 2004, 2015 by Tyndale House Foundation. Used by permission of Tyndale House Publishers, Inc., Carol Stream, Illinois 60188. All rights reserved.

Scripture is used from the New King James Version, © 1982 by Thomas Nelson, Inc. All rights reserved. Used by permission.

Scriptures marked KJV are taken from the KING JAMES VERSION (KJV): public domain.

Published by Carpenter's Son Publishing, Franklin, TN
Christianbookservices.com

Interior Design by Suzanne Lawing

Cover Design by Jenny Carvajal

Printed in the United States of America

ISBN: 978-1-956370-72-0 (print)

ACKNOWLEDGEMENTS

To my wife Susan- thanks for being my ride or die girl. Through all the ups and downs of our life, you've stayed by my side. I still can't believe God gave me the prettiest girl in school to be my wife and best friend. I am truly a blessed man. Thanks for your unending support and encouragement. We are a great team together. Love you Babes!

To Cassie and Lizzy my "Baby Girls"- I am so proud to call you both my daughters. As a Christian I don't believe in luck, but I can't help but 'feel lucky' to have such great girls like you. Because of you, I understand more fully God's unconditional love as a Father. You're never too grown up to hear these words, "I love you with all of my heart, no matter what, forever."

To my Dad- I'm so grateful for all you've done for me. How you sacrificially made a way for me to play the game of hockey. The practices, the equipment, the time- thank you, thank you. You instilled in me a discipline and work ethic that is still serving me and my family well till this very day. You're a great Dad, Provider and friend. I'm forever grateful to you. Love you Dad!

To my Mom- thanks for being the spiritual catalyst for our entire family. Our eternity was forever changed because you decided to say yes to Jesus. I know it wasn't always easy, but the Lord took your small steps of faithfulness and altered the lives of so many. It really is incredible. By the way, everyone knows you're awesome, except you! You're a great Mom and loved by all. Thank you and I love you more than you could ever know!

To Pastor Ron Lewis (The Bishop)- thanks for being a mentor and a friend all these years. I remember early on in our relationship asking, "Why does this guy even like me?" I'm still trying to figure it out. Thanks for showing me that faith can be fun! Wherever you go there is always laughter and joy. Thanks for teaching me about the Grace of God-His unmerited favor and smile. You're a hero to me bro! Much love and thanks!

FOREWORD

By Pastor Ron Lewis

Over breakfast in the late 90's, while reading the *Raleigh News & Observer,* I was thrilled to find out that a professional hockey team, newly named the Carolina Hurricanes, was relocating to our city from Hartford, Connecticut.

While reading this news I had a spiritual sense that I'd somehow be connected to this new team. A few days later, John Blue, a former goalie for the Boston Bruins, called to ask if I'd reach out to his friend and fellow hockey player, Adam Burt, defenceman for the Hurricanes.

I somewhat reluctantly called Adam, and remarkably, he answered. Not expecting an answer, I blurted out, "Hey Adam, welcome to Raleigh, how can I serve you?" The silent pause felt like an hour, then I heard him holler to his wife, "Susan, there's a pastor on the phone and he says he can serve us."

Turns out Adam was juggling multiple things having just moved his life and family to Raleigh. What began with airport runs, then meals together, became family friends and eventually lifelong ministry partners.

A few months after our first introduction, I asked Adam if he wanted to join me to speak at one of our campus ministries. Beginning his message that night I was surprised to notice this NHL'er who played before thousands every night, was actually nervous.

No one else saw it though, and Adam's first message was exceptional. He told that group of college students about being hit by a puck and for many days after seeing double. He compared his story to a message from Scripture saying, "A double minded man is unstable in all his ways."

Adam Burt the hockey player was clearly a leader, naturally gifted speaker, and to this day one of the best story tellers anywhere. We both sensed a second calling to come for him post hockey, one that would merge our lives even more deeply and demand a new kind of endurance for both of us.

While Adam was looking ahead and preparing for this next career of being a minister, he was still on the ice taking a barrage of hits, bruises and scars.

I'll never forget one of the calls I got from Susan. "Adam took a point-blank puck to the face," she told me. "He's got a bunch of stitches and is looking rough, but he'll be ok." Susan was always incredibly strong in these moments, and I thought I was too, until Adam walked into the living room. Standing upright with his usual perfect posture, he gave a slight smile. What I saw shook me to the core as I held back tears. Half of his face was caved in like Arnold Schwarznegger at the end of *Terminator 2*.

That was one of the worst injuries, but not the only or the last. I've marveled watching him overcome so many injuries and physical pain — More than 200 stitches, a broken jaw, a broken nose (several times), two cheekbone reconstructions, a knee reconstruction, a shoulder dislocation, five back surgeries, with multiple screws and plates holding together his internal skeleton. Strength of body, soul and spirit have helped this man endure.

After 14 years as a pro hockey player, Adam hung up his skates with great accolades and a deep calling to go into full-time ministry. His last game was at the iconic Madison Square Garden in midtown Manhattan. It was poetic justice that precisely one year later, he was preaching in the pulpit of the Lamb's Theater, on West 44th Street, exactly 10 blocks away from that final game.

Adam is just as facile with pulpits as with pucks, and with the help of our NYC based team, he helped launch one church in Manhattan and another just across the Hudson River in northern New Jersey, which he leads until this day.

The pain he absorbed as an athlete was not wasted and God has recycled his suffering to embrace countless pain-filled lives in New York City and in New Jersey. Adam the player became Adam the coach, the confidant, the shepherd and the teammate…to actors, Wall Street investors, Broadway celebrities, NYPD cops and NYFD firemen. A long-time chaplain for the NY Jets NFL team, Adam Burt has made an extraordinary impact for Christ in the most influential city in the world.

The secret to his giftedness in ministry is that just like on the ice, he's raw and real. Deeply grounded in biblical theology he makes you laugh one minute, and cry the next. His gifts of talent, heart, and intellect have helped countless souls find their way to the grace and mercy of God.

While my first phone call was an offer to serve him, Adam has stood by me in some of my darkest personal moments….a painful divorce, the loss of my 23 yr old son, and in happier times as a groomsman in my wedding and true co-laborer in the tough but rewarding fabric of NYC.

His life exemplifies true grit, true loyalty, and true discipleship. He's relatable, hilarious, pursues underdogs to build them up, and is faithful to the core. He'll never give up on a friend or his family. As you read this book, I'm certain you'll love getting to know his heart and deep insights like I do, and that the pain through which he's persevered will benefit you too. This book will help you get to know God and discover your God-given purpose. I couldn't put it down.

CONTENTS

INTRODUCTION 15

SECTION 1: "MISSING THE MARK: ANSWERING LIFE'S BIG QUESTIONS"

CHAPTER 1	"WHO AM I?" (IDENTITY) 25
CHAPTER 2	"WHY AM I HERE?" (PURPOSE) 35
CHAPTER 3	"WHAT'S WRONG WITH THE WORLD?" (SIN) 45
CHAPTER 4	"HOW CAN IT BE FIXED?" (THE CROSS/THE GOSPEL) 55

SECTION 2: "TRAINING TO WIN"

CHAPTER 5	"GAME PLAN" (THE BIBLE) 77
CHAPTER 6	"TALKING WITH THE GREAT ONE" (PRAYER) 89
CHAPTER 7	"POWER" (THE HOLY SPIRIT) 99
CHAPTER 8	"TEAMMATES" (THE CHURCH) 113

SECTION 3: "PLAYING TO WIN"

| CHAPTER 9 | "HOW TO PLAY THE GAME" (LOVE GOD AND LOVE PEOPLE) . . . . . .135 |
| CHAPTER 10 | "ONE SHIFT AT A TIME" (FAITH AND REPENTANCE) . . . . 149 |

CHAPTER 11	"CROWD NOISE" (CHRISTIAN COURAGE AND HEAVEN'S APPLAUSE) 167
CHAPTER 12	"MAKE YOUR LAST GAME YOUR BEST GAME" (TAKE YOUR SHOT) 187
ENDNOTES	195

INTRODUCTION

I played this game a million times over in my head. As a kid growing up in Detroit, my driveway doubled as some of the world's most iconic hockey venues. There I am, on the ice. Of course the game is tied. I can hear the roaring crowds, my teammates shouting, and then the play by play in my mind: "It's the Stanley Cup playoffs, sudden death overtime! Adam Burt has the puck as the time is ticking down. Three, two, one . . . he shoots . . . HE SCORES!!" It always ends the same. We win!

It's funny how real life is always a bit more complicated than that. Fast-forward several years later, I was about a decade into my NHL career, playing for the Philadelphia Flyers. Our team was stacked with All-stars and future Hall of Famers. We had a solid year, clinching first place in the final game of the regular season. We rolled through our first round playoff opponent, the Buffalo Sabres, winning the best of seven series four games to one.

Our next opponent was our in-state rival, the Pittsburgh Penguins. We dropped the first two games on home ice, leaving our team and fans stunned. The series headed back to Pittsburgh for games three and four. Game three was a back and forth battle. At the end of regulation the score was knotted up at 3, and we went to sudden death overtime. Next goal wins. In my driveway as a kid, I don't recall being quite as nervous as I was in real life—like, I might throw up kinda nervous. This was way more intense than I could have imagined. The game ping-ponged back and forth. Finally at 11:01 of the first overtime, my defense partner, rookie Andy Delmore, rifled a shot from the point and scored! We won and were right back in the series.

Two nights later, we were back at it for game four. It's a night I will never, ever forget. The game itself took seven hours to complete. It started at 7:35 p.m. and didn't finish until 2:35 a.m. (For the record, my wife fell asleep during the game!) A regulation hockey game is three periods long. We played eight and a half periods. Almost three complete games. It would become an "ESPN Classic" and go down in the record books as the longest game in the modern era.

The game was a tight checking affair, and at the end of regulation we were tied at one goal apiece. When you're on the ice, everything is happening so fast you don't have time to be nervous or think about what's at stake. But in between periods, during the intermission, that's when you had to keep your nerves in check. There was a tug-of-war going on in my head. I wanted to be the hero pretty bad, but equally as bad, I didn't want to be the guy that screwed up and lost the game for us.

The first overtime intermission was extremely tense. The locker room was silent. Eerily silent. Each player knew one mistake could cost us the game and possibly the series. That silence was broken by forward Keith Jones. Keith was a great teammate and leader, but he despised working out and lifting weights. He had the body to prove it: a "dad bod." As shirtless Keith Jones rose to his feet, he announced to the room, "Men, I have something to say." All eyes locked on Keith. He panned the room to be sure he had everyone's attention and declared, *"It's official . . . I've decided I'm going to start working out next season!"* The room erupted in laughter. The tension broke. It was as if someone gave us permission to have fun again. The weight lifted, and we were free to play our game.

As the game progressed well into the night, several of our key players were violently cramping due to dehydration. Our locker room looked more like an *emergency room*. The training staff hung IV bags as some players received intravenous fluids. Not only were guys getting tired, we were getting *hungry*. Our training staff eventually had to order a dozen pizzas during one of the intermissions. I imagine the pizza deliver guy would have thought a dozen pizzas at 1:00 a.m. was going to a frat party, not to an NHL playoff game! Who knew a plain cheese pie could ever taste so good.

I believe it was Hall of Fame football coach Vince Lombardi who said, "Fatigue makes cowards of us all." Fatigue was setting in, and exhaustion was trying to rob us of our will to win. How you handle moments like that determines whether you win or lose. Will you GIVE IN? Or will you GO ALL IN? I don't remember who started it, but one by one players looked to their right and left and asked the guy next to them one simple question, "Do you need to be anywhere tonight?" To which each man responded, "Nope. I got nowhere else I'd rather be. I can play all night if that's what it takes! Let's go!" At that moment, I knew we were all in. We were going to win or die trying.

Finally, at roughly 2:35 a.m, after five and a half periods of sudden death overtime, center Keith Primeau grabbed the puck and skated up ice with a full head of steam. He crossed over into the Pittsburgh zone, eluding one defender and then another. The game seemed to go all *Matrix* like into slow motion. He let a shot fly. The puck whizzed by the Pittsburgh net minder and hit the metal crossbar of the goal. To this day I can still hear the deafening "PING!" the puck made when it hit the crossbar and dropped over the goal line. It was over! We won! Our entire team flooded onto the ice to celebrate. The exhausted Pittsburgh fans and players exited the arena in defeat, while we all hugged and high-fived one another. What a moment. As I left the ice to head back into our dressing room, a profound sense of gratitude started to well up inside of me. It was tangible, overwhelming. I had been a part of something significant, something historic.

Back in the locker room the victory celebration continued with Gatorade baths and several superlatives that probably aren't appropriate for this book. Before taking off my sweat-soaked equipment, I looked around the room at each player, physically exhausted, yet strangely energized. It was then I realized how deeply soul satisfying it is to give everything you have and come out on top. To battle and to bleed. To pour every ounce of strength into something you believe in. Afterwards, you can look your teammates in the eye and honestly say, "I left it all out there for you. I held nothing back." There is something powerful and real when you can do that. It's almost spiritual. I want that for you.

You may never lace up a pair of skates or put on a hockey jersey. But make no mistake about it. You are a part of an epic game—the *game of life*. Nobody knows how long their game will last. We can only take it moment by moment, day by day. Living each moment as if it were your last, holding nothing back. And when it's your time, there will be this deafening "PING!" The game will be over. You will stand before your Creator and, I pray, you will be able to look into His glorious face and say, "I left it all out there for you. I held nothing back." In that moment, all the ridiculous things we think are so important will fade into the background of eternity as you hear these words: *"Well done, My good and faithful servant. Enter into your Master's joy."* I want that for you. I want you to win in the game of life.

A few short years after that epic game, I was forced to retire due to multiple back surgeries. What was next in the game of life for me? Broadcasting? Business? Have you ever heard the saying, *"If you want to make God laugh, tell Him your plans"*? Pastoring a church was not on my radar. In fact, early in my NHL career, a local newspaper did an article on me and my Christian faith. (Back in my day, to find a Christian in the NHL was rare. I mean, you were more likely to find a unicorn or an Oompa Loompa than find a Christian in the NHL.) The article ended with something my wife and I still laugh about to this day, "Maybe Adam will be a pastor someday." To which my wife replied, "I will never be married to a pastor!" SURPRISE!! I became a pastor. (By the way, never tell God what you won't do.)

In 2003, I helped start a church in Manhattan, alongside my pastor and mentor Ron Lewis. The church grew, and I grew along with it. Several years into my tenure at the church, one of the New York Jets football players showed up on a Sunday morning. He was a massive man and stood out among the normal crowd. I introduced myself and asked his name. "Kenyon Coleman," he replied. After the service, Kenyon approached me and suggested something I never saw coming: "You should be our team's chaplain." I was stunned and a bit skeptical, but I gave him my number. Honestly, afterwards I didn't think much about it.

A few days later, I received a call from one of the New York Jets coaches. He invited me to come and "try out" for the team chaplaincy role. Try out? How do you try out to be an NFL football chaplain? Just think *American Idol* for pastors? I was brought in to the team's facility along with a few other "contestants." We had to preach our best sermon to a handful of Jet's players and then they voted on their favorite. See what I mean by *American Idol*? Apparently I did all right because I got the gig and have been with the Jets for the past 16 seasons.

I mention all this not to "humble-brag" but to highlight the unique and unusual path God has laid out for me. This journey has afforded me a front row seat to the greatest athletes on the planet. NHL and NFL athletes are the top 1 percent in the world, the very best at what they do. And yet I have witnessed that, for all the fame and fortune that comes along with pro sports, it can never fully satisfy the human heart. We were created for something far bigger. We were created for a relationship with God. It's how we win in the game of life. I want that for you. I want you to win.

This book will be broken down into three sections. In section 1, "Missing the Mark," we will look for answers to life's most important questions. Section 2, "Training to Win," will explore the nonnegotiables of playing the game of life. "Playing to Win," section 3, examines strategies for getting into the game.

SECTION 1

"MISSING THE MARK: ANSWERING LIFE'S BIG QUESTIONS"

*I press toward the mark for the prize of the
high calling of God in Christ Jesus.
(Philippians 3:14 KJV)*

I've heard it said, "The worst kind of failure is succeeding at the wrong thing." I think Olympic rifleman Matt Emmons would agree. During the 2004 Olympic Games in Athens, Greece, Emmons held a commanding lead and was cruising towards gold in the 50-meter three-position event. Facing the final target, he eyed the mark and took a deep breath. He exhaled and pulled the trigger. BULLSEYE! The crowd's reaction, however, didn't quite fit the moment. Rather than hearing cheers there was a gasp! He hit the target dead center, but it wasn't his target. It was his competitor's. Emmons plummeted to eighth place and lost the gold medal.

This story does have a silver lining. Later that evening, Matt went out to a local pub in the Olympic Village to drown his sorrows. As he ordered a pint, another Olympian sat down at the bar beside him and offered a few words of consolation. HER name was Katarina Kurkova from the Czech National sharpshooting team. The two hit it off, and a few short years later they were married. He lost the gold, but got the girl! [1]

Missing the mark hits a little too close to home for me. I missed the net. A WIDE open net! It was during the longest game, and to this day, I mentally replay that moment over and over again. It was midway through the fourth overtime. Teammate Keith Manderville brought the puck into the Pittsburgh zone, drawing two defenders to himself. I jumped into the rush, and somehow the puck found its way onto my stick. The goaltender was out of position, I had a wide-open net. The game was mine to win. I was going to score and be the hero. The only thing I could NOT DO was miss the net. I missed the net.

Missing the net in a game is tough. But missing the mark in life is devastating. It can happen to the best of us. The Apostle Paul was one of those guys. He was excelling at all the wrong things. Aiming his life at the wrong target. He was religiously checking all the boxes. As he says in his own words, he was:

circumcised on the eighth day, of the people of Israel, of the tribe of Benjamin, a Hebrew of Hebrews; as to the law, a Pharisee; as to zeal, a persecutor of the church; as to righteousness under the law, blameless. (Philippians 3:5-6 ESV)

Winning at the wrong things left him empty, self-righteous and hard hearted. He admits:

I was formerly a blasphemer, a persecutor, and a violent man. (1 Timothy 1:13 BSB)

But something happened on a Damascus road. He had an encounter with Jesus Christ, and his life would never be the same. It was a miraculous course correction. Setting his sights on a new target. Paul says:

I press toward the mark for the prize of the high calling of God in Christ Jesus. (Philippians 3:14 ESV)

And with a refocusing of his life, Paul would absolutely change the world. Stop for a moment on your own road and ask this question: Are you aiming at the right mark?

I'm a huge fan of the game show *Family Feud*. You've probably seen it, so you know host Steve Harvey is hilarious and tells it like it is. One particular episode stands out to me. Harvey begins with his usual, "Top five answers on the board," and then he poses the question, "Name something that begins with the word 'pork.'"

The contestant immediately chimes in, "Cupine, Steve!" Harvey looks a bit confused, "What?" Undeterred, the contestant confidently repeats, "Cupine, Steve!" Harvey is like, "What is a 'Cupine'?" The contestant puffs out his chest and replies like he is Albert Einstein, "Cupine, Steve… 'Pork-Cupine'…..you know, like a 'porcupine.'"

Harvey's bewildered look is priceless. And then, right on cue, the contestant's team responds the way they always do . . . THEY LIE! "Good answer! Good answer!" No, it's not! It's a dumb answer and everyone knows it. Steve can't help himself and says as much: "You're the only one that thinks that's a good answer." The team then doubles down on the dumb answer and says, "It's up there, Steve! It's gonna be up there!" Surprisingly, he agrees, "It's gonna be up there all right . . . on YouTube because it's so dumb!" If you were wondering? No, it wasn't on the board. It was a dumb answer. [2]

Is it just me, or are there some really dumb answers being thrown around today? Some of life's most difficult questions are getting "Cupine!" answers. They're dumb, but for some reason we feel all this pressure to agree and applaud, "Good Answer, Good Answer." I truly believe there is only one "Good Answer" to life's biggest questions and that answer is Jesus.

I'm not saying every other answer is completely wrong. But if you're "kinda wrong" or completely wrong, does it really matter? Either way, you are wrong.

C. S. Lewis highlights my point:

> If you are a Christian you do not have to believe that all the other religions are simply wrong all through. If you are an atheist you do have to believe that the main point in all the religions of the whole world is simply one huge mistake. If you are a Christian, you are free to think that all these religions, even the queerest ones, contain at least some hint of the truth. When I was an atheist I had to try to persuade myself that most of the human race have always been wrong about the question that mattered to them most; when I became a Christian I was able to take a more liberal view. But, of course, being a Christian does mean thinking that where Christianity differs from other religions, Christianity is right and they are wrong. As in arithmetic—there is only one right answer to a sum, and all other answers are wrong: but some of the wrong answers are much nearer being right than others. [3]

Deep down inside, all of us are asking some version of these four questions:

1. Who am I?

2. Why am I here?

3. What's wrong with the world?

4. How can it be fixed?

In the marketplace of ideas, I believe Christianity answers these four questions best. It's hitting life's "bullseye." In section one, we will tackle each of these four questions in separate chapters. In the end, I hope and pray you too will come to the same conclusion. Jesus is the answer. I want you to hit your mark. I want you to win in the game of life.

CHAPTER 1

"WHO AM I?" (IDENTITY)

But the evil spirit answered them, "Jesus I know, and Paul I recognize, but who are you?" (Acts 19:15 ESV)

Who are you? It's a question I won't soon forget. Our team was on another road trip. The routine was always the same: flight, hotel, dinner and then MASSAGE! Oh, how I miss the pregame massage. In Philadelphia, we had one of the best massage therapists in the entire NHL. His name was Tommy. He had long black hair he kept pulled back in a ponytail. He was super strong and seemed to have endless energy as he worked on one player after another. Tommy was a spiritual guy, but not a Christian. We would have spiritual conversations occasionally, as he worked on sore, knotted muscles. This particular evening, I remember being on the massage table, not really wanting to talk at all. I was in the dumps, feeling kind of sorry for myself. My play on the ice had been less than stellar, and I was letting it get the best of me.

Lying on my back, I was literally almost asleep on the table, when the massage came to a screeching halt. Tommy stopped massaging and started pounding his clenched fist onto my chest like he was beating a drum. He got right up in my face and started yelling, "Who are you? Who are you? Who are you?" Honestly, I wasn't sure if Tommy was tripping or was having a PTSD episode or something similar. Again he demanded, "Who are you?" "Tommy!……It's me!.. Adam…..it's me!" "No!" He paused and then whispered, "You are a child of God." He immediately resumed the massage, as if nothing had happened. It was a bizarre moment for sure. But for me, it really landed. God spoke to Moses through a burning bush and to Balaam through a donkey. I guess God can speak to me through a massage therapist. *"I am a child of God."* Who are you?

FAKE ID'S

Who are you? The identity question is a big one! If you don't answer it, someone else will answer it for you: You are your *sexuality*. You are your *bank account*. You are your *looks*. You are your career. The list goes on and on. Who are you?

Have you ever had a fake ID? I know, as Christians, we don't do such things, but just pretend, hypothetically, that I obtained one as a seventeen-year-old kid in order to buy beer while underage. OK, it wasn't actually hypothetical. Don't judge me! The fake ID read: Scott Livinston, Height 5'10," blond hair, blue eyes. Which is somewhat problematic because I am six feet two inches with brown hair and brown eyes.

I remember the first time I actually tried to use it. I nervously grabbed a case of beer. (Don't worry, it wasn't light beer.) I approached the checkout counter. The guy looked me up and down and then asked to see my ID. I sheepishly handed it to him. He looked down at the ID and then back at me. Again, he looked at the ID and back at me. He handed it back and said these three words: "That's not YOU."

If you are building your identity on your looks, your sexuality, or your bank account, I want to reiterate those same three words: *"That's not you."* They are fake ID's. Building your identity on these temporary things will make you extremely fragile. You become vulnerable to the onslaught of circumstances everyday life throws at you.

For example, if you build your identity on your wealth, what happens if you lose your wealth? Who are you then? Solomon the wealthiest man who ever lived wrote this:

Do not toil to acquire wealth; be discerning enough to desist. When your eyes light on it, it is gone, for suddenly it sprouts wings, flying like an eagle toward heaven. (Proverbs 23:4-5 ESV)

I've seen this verse played out in real time. I was with an NFL Hall of Fame wide receiver the day he learned he had been swindled out of nine million dollars in a Ponzi scheme by a man you may have heard of, Bernie Madoff! Everything he had worked so hard to attain vanished. Gone in an instant. Don't build your identity on your wealth. Your money can sprout wings and be taken from you. Then, you not only lose your money, you lose your identity.

Who are you? Some people build their identity on their looks. Their entire sense of self-worth is wrapped up in their beauty. Is this you? What happens if you lose your hair? What if you're disfigured in an accident or simply grow old? With every gray hair, line, or wrinkle you will slowly begin to die a million deaths. As your beauty fades, so does your sense of self. Now who are you? Do you see how fragile life becomes when you build your sense of worth and identity on these fake ID's? When you secure your identity to insecure things your life also becomes insecure and fragile. I believe Christianity offers a more robust answer to the identity question. You can secure your identity to something enduring and unchanging, something eternal. To answer the question, "Who am I?" We have to go back to the beginning, the very beginning.

> *In the beginning, God created the heavens and the earth.*
> *(Genesis 1:1 ESV)*

In Genesis 1, we read that God creates the world in six days. There is a rhythm and pattern to the creation narrative: God creates and declares, "It's good," God creates and declares, "It's good," God creates and declares, "It's good." Six times God repeats this pattern. (Only one day in the creation narrative doesn't receive an "It's good" from the Lord. Do you know which day? Day Two. It's a Monday! When your alarm goes off Monday morning for work, it definitely won't feel good.)

We can deduce at least two critical truths about the character and nature of God from this rhythm in creation:

- **#1 God is good.** Everything He creates is good. Therefore God must be good. The creation reveals something about the Creator.

- **#2 Work is good.** There is something spiritual and rewarding about working hard and then stepping back to enjoy what you've produced. It's good. This speaks to purpose, which we will tackle in depth in chapter 2.

But let's get back to the identity question, "Who are you?" We get our answer in Genesis 1:26:

> *Then God said, "Let us make man in our image, after our likeness. And let them have dominion over the fish of the sea and over the birds of the heavens and over the livestock and over all the earth and over every creeping thing that creeps on the earth."*
> *(Genesis 1:26 ESV)*

Your Primary Identity is an "image bearer of God." It's God's design for mankind. You and I are unique and distinct in all the created order. We've been created "in God's image." The New Testament will take it a step further and declare, in Christ, you are a son or daughter of God:

But to all who did receive him [Jesus], who believed in his name, he gave the right to become children of God. (John 1:12 ESV)

Knowing who you are and where you are from becomes the firm foundation to build your life upon.

For most of his life, Deland McCullough felt a massive void in his soul. This gnawing question haunted him: "Who are my biological parents?" Adopted as an infant, Deland grew increasingly more frustrated over his lack of answers. He would channel that frustration onto the football field, which served him well. College recruiters from top universities took their shot at landing young Deland. One recruiter from Miami University in Ohio, stood out. His name was Sherman Smith. It wasn't just the fact that he rolled up in a sweet Mercedes-Benz. There was something magnetic about this man. After he talked with Sherman Smith, Deland was sold and committed to Miami of Ohio to play football. He excelled on the field, setting new school records and was hopeful he'd get a shot at the NFL. Deland went undrafted, but signed as a free agent with the Cincinnati Bengals. Several knee injuries eventually ended his brief NFL career. What was next?

Deland's next move would be in the coaching world. He followed in the footsteps of his mentor and former coach, Sherman Smith. Smith, now with the Seattle Seahawks, offered Deland an internship with the team. It quickly became evident he'd be an excellent football coach one day. Although many of Deland's career questions were being answered, the question that he couldn't shake—where he had actually come from—still went unanswered.

Fast-forward several years later, the adoption laws were amended, enabling Deland to pursue the identity of his birth parents. First, he found his birth mom, Carol Briggs. She often wondered about her son. Would she ever meet him? How did his life turn out? With Deland's personal search for his identity, her questions, too, would soon be answered. Deland arranged a meeting via phone. The reunited mother and son ping-ponged questions back and forth to one another. Carol explained how she got pregnant as a teenager. She never even told the father of her pregnancy. He was just a kid as well. She could barely care for herself, let alone a newborn child. Adoption seemed the best solution. Deland, trying to process all this information, asked the next logical question, "Who is my father?" She paused and replied, "Your father's name is Sherman Smith." Mic drop! Deland was speechless, almost breathless. His former coach, mentor, and friend was actually his father. [1]

In an ESPN *E60* interview, Deland delivers what I believe to be the "money line" of his story: "Now I know who I am and where I'm from ….I got all the pieces to the story." Do you know who you are? Do you have all the pieces to life's ultimate story?

Who are you? You are an image bearer of God. If you've received Jesus' work on the cross, you are a child of God. That's your *Primary Identity*. Do you see how rock solid that is? That identity is unchanging and eternal. It can never be taken from you. It will never, ever change. "Child of God" becomes the firm foundation on which to build your life. With that as your *Primary Identity* you can withstand anything life may throw at you.

Now, with your *Primary Identity* settled, you have something solid to build all of your *Secondary Identities* upon. What are these Secondary Identities? I'll use myself as an example. I have a myriad of *Secondary Identities* and so do you. I'm a man. I'm a father, a son, a husband. I'm a pastor. The list goes on and on. If I make any of these Secondary Identities, primary, I make myself vulnerable to life's unforeseen circumstances. Secondary Identities are temporal and can be taken from you in an instant. For example, I was once an NHL hockey player. It would have been so easy to make that my *Primary Identity*, but it's fragile and temporary. I was forced to retire from the NHL at age thirty-three after several back surgeries. At the time I wondered, now who am I? You see what I mean about being fragile? Vulnerable?

If I'm not a hockey player, who am I? But, if my *Primary Identity* is child of God and my *Secondary Identity* is an NHL hockey player. I can lose my career as an NHLer without losing who I am. Do you see how much security and stability that adds to my life?

Our Primary Identity should inform all of our Secondary identities. For me, child of God (Primary Identity) informs how I live and act as a father, a husband, a friend, an employee (Secondary Identities). Who you think you are will determine what you do. Your identity determines your activity. As you see your life through the lens of image bearer and child of God, you will become the very best version of "You" that you can be.

Below is a simple diagram I hope you find helpful.

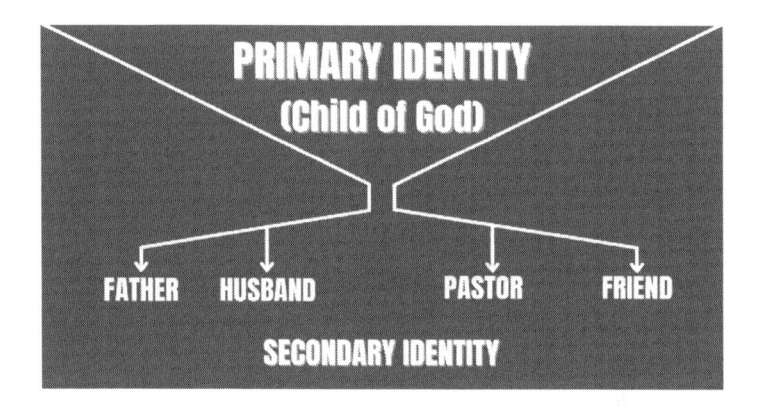

PRIMARY IDENTITY
(Child of God)

FATHER   HUSBAND   PASTOR   FRIEND

SECONDARY IDENTITY

IDENTITY THEFT

On average, roughly nine million Americans per year will be a victim of identity theft.[2]

The Bible is clear, we have a mortal enemy. He is called by several names: Satan, the Devil, the Father of Lies. Jesus calls him a "Thief"

"The thief comes only to steal and kill and destroy. I came that they may have life and have it abundantly." (John 10:10 ESV)

What does Satan come to steal? Your identity. If he can get your identity, he can control your activity. Satan's first attack on Adam and Eve was an assault on their identity.

Now the serpent was more crafty than any other beast of the field that the LORD God had made. He said to the woman, "Did God actually say, 'You shall not eat of any tree in the garden'?" And the woman said to the serpent, "We may eat of the fruit of the trees in the garden, but God said, 'You shall not eat of the fruit of the tree that is in the midst of the garden, neither shall you touch it, lest you die.'" But the serpent said to the woman, "You will not surely die. For God knows that when you eat of it your eyes will be opened, and you will be like God, knowing good and evil.
(Genesis 3:1-5 ESV)

Did you catch the lie? "You will be like God." They already were like God. They were created in His image. Eve forgot who she was. She forgot her Primary Identity and it cost her everything.

In Matthew, God the Father answers the identity question for His Son:

And when Jesus was baptized, immediately he went up from the water, and behold, the heavens were opened to him, and he saw the Spirit of God descending like a dove and coming to rest on him; and behold, a voice from heaven said, "This is my beloved Son, with whom I am well pleased." (Matthew 3:16-17 ESV)

Who are you Jesus? You are the "beloved Son" of God (Primary Identity). Immediately after this defining moment, Jesus goes into the wilderness to be tempted by the Devil. The very first attack on Jesus was an assault on His Primary Identity:

And after fasting forty days and forty nights, He was hungry. And the tempter came and said to him, "If you are the Son of God, command these stones to become loaves of bread."
(Matthew 4:2-3 ESV)

"IF *you are the Son of God?*" The audible voice of God just settled that question. Jesus IS the "beloved Son" of God. Satan knows that if he can rob Jesus of His identity, he can control His activity. Satan is coming for your identity. Do you know who you are?

I'll end this chapter with the seven sons of Sceva. We read about them in Acts 19. These seven sons were Jewish exorcists. They had seen the profound power displayed by the Apostle Paul through Christ, power to heal the sick and to cast out demons. These seven men were hired to cast a demon out of a man.

The seven sons of Sceva boldly spoke to the demon possessed man, "We adjure you by the Jesus whom Paul proclaims!" Brace yourself, because the Bible says the demon responded!

> *But the evil spirit answered them, "Jesus I know, and Paul I recognize, but <u>who are you?</u>" And the man in whom was the evil spirit leaped on them, mastered all of them and overpowered them, so that they fled out of that house naked and wounded. (Acts 19:15-16 ESV)*

When a demon possessed person asks, "Who are you?" You better know the answer to that question!

CHAPTER 2

"WHY AM I HERE?" (PURPOSE)

"For David, after he had served the purpose of God in his own generation, fell asleep." (Acts 13:36 ESV)

CHOSEN FOR A PURPOSE

The 1987 NHL entry draft was held in my hometown of Detroit, Michigan. What an exciting and nerve-racking time. All those years of practice and hard work were culminating in this moment. My entire family was there, nervously waiting for my name to be called. It was the late '80s, so the mullet was cool. You remember the mullet, right? Business in the front and party in the back. I was wearing it proudly. My draft day outfit was a cream-colored jacket with a pink pastel shirt and a blue knit tie. If *Miami Vice* and *The Fresh Prince of Bel-Air* had a baby, that's how it would be dressed.

Despite my lack of fashion sense, the selection continued. The 39th pick finally came along. It belonged to the Hartford Whalers. Hartford's General Manager approached the podium to make the selection. "The Hartford Whalers select… with the thirty-ninth overall pick, from the

North Bay Centennials of the Ontario Hockey League…Adam Burt." I walked down from the crowded stands to my new GM and shook his hand. He presented me with my new uniform. I slid the jersey over my head. At that moment, I became a Hartford Whaler. I was chosen. Chosen for a purpose. The Apostle Paul writes:

In Him [Jesus] we were also chosen as God's own, having been predestined according to the plan of Him who works out everything by the counsel of His will, in order that we, who were the first to hope in Christ, would be for the praise of His glory.
(Ephesians 1:11-12 BSB)

I pray you feel a deep sense of meaning and purpose as an image bearer of God. Just like my name was called out at the draft, you too have been chosen for a great destiny and purpose. It's time to stop being a spectator in the game of life.

February 20, 2020. The Carolina Hurricanes were in Toronto to take on the Maple Leafs. The Canes took an early 3–1 lead, when the unthinkable happened. They ran out of goaltenders! Both of Carolina's netminders were injured during the contest. The NHL has a rather bizarre rule. In the event a team loses both goalies, the home team must provide an emergency goaltender to fill in. This replacement can play for either team. The emergency goaltender for this game was forty-two-year-old David Ayres. He drove the zamboni (the machine that cleans the ice in between periods) for the Maple Leafs' minor league affiliate. The announcer called his name, and, looking stunned and not a little nervous, Ayers hurried out of the stands and into the game with 8:41 left in the second period. The first two shots he faced went in!

Somehow, Ayers was able to compose himself and managed to stop the remaining eight shots of the game. Amid roaring fans on both sides of the arena, the Carolina Hurricanes went on to win 6–3. The victorious zamboni driver was named the game's first star, and the Hurricanes celebrated the win by showering him with water and cheers. Ayers would become the oldest goalie to win his NHL debut, and the stick he used that incredible night was added to the Hockey Hall of Fame. [1]

Can you imagine? Ayers was just sitting in the stands, watching the contest, when he was called out of the crowd and into the game. Are you a spectator in the game of life? Or have you answered the call to enter the game?

I remember the first time I truly realized that I have a role to play in the game of life. A friend and former NHL goaltender, John Blue, had recently retired and become a minister. We were discussing life and faith over a couple of Starbucks lattes when he hit me with a question that would literally change the trajectory of my life: "What are you doing for the Kingdom of God?" I very quickly and defensively responded, "I read my Bible. I love my wife and kids. I go to church." He quickly volleyed back, "I didn't ask you about your morality. I asked you, what are you DOING for the Kingdom of God?" Honestly, he pissed me off a bit. He struck a nerve, and I'm so glad he did. That day I saw for the first time that the Christian life is far bigger than just trying to be a good person until you die or until Christ returns. God has a mission and purpose for your life. We don't have to be spectators. We are all called to play in the game of life.

I believe it was Mark Twain who said, *"The two most important days in your life are the day you were born and the day you find out why."* That day as I talked with John I started getting clarity on my purpose. I pray today is that day for you. Do you know your purpose?

DIVINE DESIGN

In chapter 1, we answered the question "Who am I?" You are an image bearer of God, and through Christ a son or daughter of God. As an image bearer, you've been uniquely designed to reflect God's image. Remember, your identity determines your activity. Therefore, your purpose is inextricably tied to your identity. God's purpose for you is to reflect His image and glorify Him wherever you go and whatever you do.

In Genesis we read:

The earth was without form and void, and darkness was over the face of the deep. And the Spirit of God was hovering over the face of the waters. (Genesis 1:2 ESV)

Afterwards, God goes to work and starts to form it and fill it. Pay attention to that pattern of forming and filling. On days one through three of creation, God forms "the expanse of the heavens above and the earth below. He separates the waters from the dry ground." He creates the perfect atmosphere for life and flourishing. Then, on days four through six He fills it with life, "the birds of the air, the fish of the sea and the beasts of the field." Finally on day six, God creates His masterpiece! His image bearer:

Then the LORD God formed the man of dust from the ground and breathed into his nostrils the breath of life, and the man became a living creature. (Genesis 2:7 ESV)

God formed mankind from dust and filled us with the breath of life. The rest of creation God spoke into existence with a word, but not mankind. We were not formed with words alone. For us, God got His hands dirty. You are a very unique blend of heaven and earth. There is a humility that should mark all of us, since we are formed from dust. And yet, there is an inherent dignity that distinguishes us from the rest of creation. We are formed in His image and filled with the breath, or the Spirit of God. This gives each of us the power to be His image bearer.

The Prophet Habakkuk will say it this way:

For the earth will be filled with the knowledge of the glory of the LORD as the waters cover the sea. (Habakkuk 2:14 ESV)

How will God's glory cover the earth? Through YOU and ME! His image bearers.

Adam and Eve were God's original image bearers. God placed them in a garden called Eden, which means "delight." (Isn't that cool?) God formed and filled this garden with beauty and delight and then gave the man and the woman their mission or purpose:

And God blessed them. And God said to them, "Be fruitful and multiply and fill the earth and subdue it, and have dominion over the fish of the sea and over the birds of the heavens and over every living thing that moves on the earth." (Genesis 1:28 ESV)

In other words, God says to make the rest of the world look like Eden. We become the image of God when we *form* families, societies, cities and institutions for human flourishing. Then we *fill it with* children, culture, art, beauty, love, security, all to the glory of God. We "Edenize" the world. What a great purpose!

Unfortunately, this time of delight, this forming and filling by Adam and Eve, only lasts for two chapters of the Bible. In Genesis 3, Adam and Eve eat of the forbidden fruit, and in essence rebel against their Creator. Sin is introduced into the world, and it corrupts God's good creation. Adam and Eve are thrust out of Eden and separated from the presence of God when that happened. We lost our Breath. We lost the Spirit. Something died on the inside of humanity. The Apostle Paul says it this way:

. . . our foolish hearts grew dark. (Romans 1:21 ESV)

As the heart of mankind grew dark, we lost the light of life and our ability to image God. We lost our purpose.

Author and podcaster Cathy Heller famously said. *"The opposite of depression is not happiness, it's purpose."* [2] I tend to agree with her and so would another guy you may have heard of, Olympic swimmer Michael Phelps. Phelps is the most decorated Olympian of all time. He won twenty-eight medals, and twenty-three of those are gold! All of that success in the pool earned him a great deal of fame and fortune. His net worth is an estimated one hundred million dollars.

Yet with all that going for him, Phelps found himself in a deep depression following the 2012 Olympics in London. He decided to retire from competitive swimming and was immediately confronted with the question, *"Who am I outside of the pool?"* This question haunted him and took him down a dark path. Alcohol seemed to numb the pain of uncertainty for a moment. But in the end, it would simply accelerate his downward spiral. Thoughts of suicide and isolation intensified. An embarrassing DUI was the final straw. Michael needed help. Family and friends persuaded the Olympian to enter a rehab facility.

A longtime friend and NFL Hall of Famer, Ray Lewis, decided to pay Phelps a visit. It was a visit that would literally save Phelps's life. Lewis, a committed Christian, gave him a copy of Rick Warren's *The Purpose Driven Life*. Phelps devoured the book. Each page was like oxygen, breathing new life back into his soul. Later, Phelps told ESPN, "It's turned me into believing there is a power greater than myself…. and there is a purpose for me on this planet." [3]

Michael found his way back to God and back to the pool! Coming out of retirement, he went on to capture five gold medals and a silver in the 2016 Olympic games in Rio. Phelps rediscovered his purpose and so can you!

BREATHE AGAIN

In the book of John, the resurrected Christ appears to His bewildered disciples and says:

> *"Peace be with you. As the Father has sent me, even so I am sending you." And when he had said this, he breathed on them and said to them, "Receive the Holy Spirit." (John 20:21-22 ESV)*

"He breathed on them." This is John's way of directing us all back to creation in Genesis where God breathed into man the breath of life. Jesus, in dying on the cross for our sins, makes it possible for us to again receive the Breath of God, the Holy Spirit! And with the Holy Spirit, we regain the power to image God. Our ability to form and fill the earth is restored. We get our purpose back.

No one can reflect God's image quite like you. You are unique.

The twenty-three chromosomes from your dad and twenty-three chromosomes from your mom make up the distinct forty-six chromosomes of your DNA. This combination is what makes you, you. The chances of you being precisely you is roughly one in one hundred trillion! You are truly one of a kind, and as such, you reflect the image of God in a unique way. The Apostle Paul would say it this way:

> *For we are his workmanship, created in Christ Jesus for good works, which God prepared beforehand, that we should walk in them. (Ephesians 2:10 ESV)*

The word "workmanship" translates to the Greek word "poiēma" which is the root word for "poem" or "poetry." You are God's poetry. His work of art. And He's created you to do "good works" or, in other words, for a purpose. David the psalmist will say it a bit more elegantly as he praises God in Psalm 139:

> *For you formed my inward parts; you knitted me together in my mother's womb. I praise you, for I am fearfully and wonderfully made. Wonderful are your works; my soul knows it very well. My frame was not hidden from you, when I was being made in secret, intricately woven in the depths of the earth. Your eyes saw my unformed substance; in your book were written, every one of them, the days that were formed for me, when as yet there was none of them. (Psalm 139:13-16 ESV)*

"Knit together in your mother's womb." "Fearfully and wonderfully made." You are a unique you, designed by God to play your part in God's story. You were created for a purpose. Not only were you uniquely designed, you've been uniquely placed by God for that purpose:

And he made from one man every nation of mankind to live on all the face of the earth, having determined allotted periods and the boundaries of their dwelling place, that they should seek God, and perhaps feel their way toward him and find him. Yet he is actually not far from each one of us. (Acts 17:26-27 ESV)

In other words, God determines where you live and when you live so that people might in some way experience God through you. God is not far from anyone because you are there! Pastor Matt Chandler says it this way: "You've been made for the day and the day was made for you." [4] I love that! As a Christian, everywhere you go and everything you do is dripping with significance and purpose. The Spirit of God is in you, to reflect the image of God through you for the glory of God and the good of people around you. I know that's a mouthful. The Apostle Paul says it more succinctly:

And whatever you do, in word or deed, do everything in the name of the Lord Jesus, giving thanks to God the Father through him. (Colossians 3:17 ESV)

Whatever you do—raising a family, working a job, going to school, playing a sport—do it in a way that glorifies God and blesses people. In Christ everything you do becomes significant and has meaning. There is no such thing as a meaningless task because you are doing it for the glory of God and the good of others. In fact, Paul says that even the smallest, most routine activities can be performed with spiritual purpose:

So, whether you eat or drink, or whatever you do, do all to the glory of God. (1 Corinthians 10:31 ESV)

Every moment is packed with purpose for the man or woman who understands that they have been created by God to bear His image each and every day. Contrast that person with the secular atheist, who answers life's big questions very, very differently. *"Who am I?"* Merely a cosmic accident, lucky mud. Some primordial soup that somehow grew into a man. *"Why am I here?"* No reason. There is no greater purpose other than to "eat, drink and be merry for tomorrow we die." These are bad answers to life's big questions, and deep down inside, we know these answers are not true. We know we've been created for so much more.

Have you ever seen *The Lion King*? It doesn't matter which version: the Broadway play, the Disney cartoon, or the major motion picture. For the record, I've seen all three. There is one scene that wrecks me every time I see it. It strikes a chord deep inside.

If you're familiar with the story, you know that Simba has a great calling and destiny to be a king. Yet because of guilt and shame, he runs from it. He's content to go through the motions and simply live like a pig. (OK, a warthog.) All that purposeless living changes when Simba meets a strange monkey, named Rafiki. Annoyed by the odd monkey, Simba asks, "Who are you anyway?" Rafiki responds, "The question is, who are you? You don't even know who you are. I know who you are. You're Mufasa's boy." Rafiki identifies Simba correctly as the son of a king. The monkey then reveals the stunning news that Mufasa isn't dead, as Simba thought.

For the first time in years, Simba feels something in his soul he thought he lost forever: Hope.

Rafiki promises to take the prince to his father. The young lion frantically follows in hopes of finding Mufasa. The pursuit ends at a body of water where Rafiki directs Simba to look into the still waters.

As he peers down into the water, all he sees is himself. In disappointment he responds, "That's just my reflection." Rafiki quickly, but softly responds, "Look harder. You see…. HE lives in you."

Simba is startled as he looks more closely, more carefully at his reflection, but this time sees his father staring back and hears his words (in the voice of the great James Earl Jones). It's these words that rock me every time: "Simba, you've forgotten me. . . . You've forgotten who you are and have therefore forgotten me. You are more than you've become. It's time for you to step up and take your place." [5]

For whatever reason, those words challenge and provoke me again and again. "You're more than you've become. It's time to step up and take your place." It reminds me that I've been created for a destiny and a purpose. I pray those words will resonate inside of you as well.

In Christ, you truly are the son or daughter of a King. In fact, He is the King of Kings. His Spirit lives inside of you. It's time for you to step up and take your place, to walk in God's destiny and purpose for your life. Do you know your purpose?

CHAPTER 3

"WHAT'S WRONG WITH THE WORLD?" (SIN)

Therefore, just as sin came into the world through one man, and death through sin, and so death spread to all men because all sinned. (Romans 5:12)

In this passage the Apostle Paul clearly points out the origins of sin and the connection between sin and death. Sin is what is wrong with the world.

FROM PEACE TO PIECES

Shattered! That was what the doctor said, after five hours of facial reconstructive surgery which included three titanium plates and about a dozen screws. The surgeon said it looked like I took a shotgun blast to the face. He was right, but it wasn't a shotgun. It was a left-hand that felt like a shotgun! At the time, I was playing for the Hartford Whalers, and we were hosting our cross state rivals the Boston Bruins.

I'll admit, Boston was a much better team than we were. They were headed to the playoffs, and we were headed to another early vacation. Mathematically eliminated from playoff contention, we were playing out the last few meaningless games of our season.

Hockey is a very unique sport. Unlike other sports that try to keep individual violence to a minimum, fist fighting is both allowed and, at times, highly strategic. There is an entire etiquette and art to a hockey fight. "You wanna go?" is hockey talk for, "Let's fight." The gloves come off and away you go. Good fighters know just where to grab their opponent and how to use balance and leverage to inflict maximum damage. I was NOT a good fighter. In fact, Hockeyfights.com (yes, there really is a website dedicated to hockey fights) said I had sixty-three fights in my NHL career. [1]

But before you go thinking I was tough, the website said I won about four of those fights!

For whatever dumb reason, I decided to drop the gloves with Boston winger Rick Tocchet. He was known around the league as an excellent fighter and good goal scorer. I was neither. The gloves flew off, and we started exchanging blows. I distinctly remember thinking to myself, "I'm doing pretty good." (FYI, it's never a good idea to think that during a fight!) Right at that moment, Tocchet threw a bomb that connected with my left cheekbone. That was the end of the fight and the end of my cheekbone. Shattered!

I tell that story, because it's our story, the human story. As you recall, Genesis 1 reveals the creation narrative. God creates with a word for the first five days. After each day, He steps back, admires His creation and declares, "It's good." On the sixth day, God gets His hands dirty and forms man from the dust of the earth. He then breathes into him the breath of life and declares, "This is very good." Afterwards, He places the man in a garden:

The LORD God took the man and placed him in the Garden of Eden in order to have him work it and guard it. (Genesis 2:15 ISV)

Now, if you're a thinker, you have to ask the question, "Guard it from what?" Wasn't this Paradise, Eden—the Garden of Delight? Later in the story, we discover there is a serpent in the Garden. A fallen angel named Lucifer. We would later know him as Satan or the Devil. More on him in a minute.

God places Adam and Eve in the Garden of Eden and tells them all of it is theirs to enjoy. Then he adds, just don't eat from one tree:

And the LORD God commanded the man, saying, "You may surely eat of every tree of the garden, but of the tree of the knowledge of good and evil you shall not eat, for in the day that you eat of it you shall surely die." (Genesis 2:16-17 ESV)

We need to pause here and pull back the lens to see something about the goodness of God. During the first six days of creation there is this constant refrain, "God creates....It was good....God creates.... It was good." Everything God creates is good. His commands are good as well. Do you remember the first two commandments from God?

#1 "Be fruitful and multiply and fill the earth and subdue it." (Genesis 1:28 ESV)

A man and his naked wife are *commanded* to be fruitful and multiply? Please don't make me explain what that entails. How good is God!

#2 "You may surely eat of every tree of the garden, but of the tree of the knowledge of good and evil you shall not eat, for in the day that you eat of it you shall surely die." (Genesis 2:16-17 ESV)

In other words, God gives us EVERYTHING there is! Except for one thing. He *commands us to enjoy it all. Just avoid the one thing.* Again, how good is God! If I could boil down the goodness of God in His creation with a single word, it would be the Hebrew word "shalom." It means "peace," but not simply in the sense of no conflict.

Its meaning is more robust, as in the sense of nothing broken and nothing lacking. And that's our story throughout Genesis 1 and 2. Shalom. There is nothing broken and nothing lacking. Perfect peace. Unfortunately, shalom is SHATTERED in Genesis 3 because of sin.

In Genesis 3, we are introduced to the Serpent:

> *Now the serpent was more crafty than any other beast of the field that the LORD God had made. He said to the woman, "Did God actually say, 'You shall not eat of any tree in the garden'?"*
> *(Genesis 3:1 ESV)*

As best we can tell from the scriptures, Lucifer was an angel in the heavenly realms. He was beautiful and spectacular. Somewhere along the line, he believed he would be a better god than God Himself. Pride entered Lucifer's heart, and he led a rebellion against the Almighty. He deceived one third of the angels and convinced them to join him in his rebellion. His ability to deceive is truly staggering. The angels, who had a front row seat to the majesty and might of God, were somehow deceived that they could, and should, overthrow Him. Lucifer and his angels rebel and are promptly defeated and cast out of heaven down to earth. From this point forward, we would no longer know the fallen angel as Lucifer. We know him as Satan or the Devil. Jesus calls him the *"father of lies"* (John 8:44).

The Serpent immediately goes to work, doing what he does best, deceiving. Do you hear the first lie and accusation against God? *"Did God actually say, 'You shall not eat of any tree in the garden'?"* God never said that. In fact, He said just the opposite. He gave them EVERYTHING except for ONE THING. Do you hear the accusation and lie about God? "God is holding out on you. Therefore, God must not be good." Have you ever heard something similar from the Father of Lies? I know I have. "If God is good, why did this happen? If God is good, why is He withholding goodness from me?" Be it a spouse, a job, or a promotion, we've all heard some version of this in our heart, but we must hear it for what it truly is, a LIE.

Eve takes the bait and believes the lie. God has given her everything there is except for *one thing* (the Tree of the Knowledge of Good and Evil). She fixates on the one thing and in doing so, will lose everything. The Devil continues:

But the serpent said to the woman, "You will not surely die. For God knows that when you eat of it your eyes will be opened, and you will be like God, knowing good and evil."(Genesis 3:4-5 ESV)

Do you see the second lie? It's an assault on her identity: "You will be like God." She was already like God. She was created "In God's image and likeness." I told you he was a good liar. Eve eats the forbidden fruit and gives it to her husband. Adam, who was to guard the Garden, instead defiles it by eating from the tree and disobeying God. Sin is introduced into our story and shalom is shattered. God's good creation is broken. God comes to Adam in the Garden:

He told the man, "Because you have listened to what your wife said, and have eaten from the tree about which I commanded you, 'You must not eat from it,' cursed is the ground because of you. You'll eat from it through pain-filled labor for the rest of your life." (Genesis 3:17 ISV)

The earth is under a curse. It's broken. I don't think you can deny it. We see the impact of sin on God's good creation immediately. In Genesis 4, Cain, Adam's firstborn son, kills Abel, his younger brother. With this first act of murder, the human condition continues a steady downward spiral from there. Death, disease, depression, and oppression ravage the world. The world is not as it should be, and we know it.

I've had my share of injuries over the course of a fourteen year NHL career. I've had roughly 200 stitches, a broken jaw, a broken nose (several times), two cheekbone reconstructions, a knee reconstruction, a shoulder dislocation, and five back surgeries—and these are just a few of the many injuries I've received playing the game I love. Honestly, I was NEVER ONCE shocked or surprised by any of them. Hockey is an extremely fast and violent sport. If you play long enough, you are going to have some scars to show for it. That's the nature of the game, and that's the nature of life in a fallen world. It's violent and dangerous. You will get dinged up. We all have the scars to prove it.

THE TRAGIC TRUTH

What's wrong with the world? Sin. I need to be clear here: We aren't simply victims of other people's sin against us. We are part of the problem as well. The early twentieth-century author and philosopher G. K. Chesterton was asked to write an article for *The Daily News* answering the question, *"What's wrong with the world?"* I love his response. He simply wrote back, "I am wrong." [2] We aren't merely victims of sin, we are perpetrators as well.

The word "sin" can be traced back to an archery term. It simply means to *"miss the mark."* All of us, in some way, shape, or form, have missed the mark God has given us.

For example, take the Ten Commandments. These commandments display the holiness of God and how life works best. Obedience to the Ten Commandments leads to life and human flourishing. If you don't believe me, let's do a little experiment. I want you to take the next thirty days and do the opposite of the Ten Commandments: lie, steal, murder, commit adultery. At the end of thirty days, let's get back together and see how your life is working out. If you're not dead, divorced, or in prison, I'd be shocked. You see, God's commandments lead us into the best life possible.

That's not all the Ten Commandments do for us. They also act as a diagnostic test to reveal the state of our hearts. Every injury I suffered playing hockey inevitably led to a visit to the hospital for an X-ray. Of course, an X-ray doesn't heal you. It simply shows you what's happening inside. The Ten Commandments do the same thing; they reveal to us that something is broken on the inside.

I want to keep God's commandments, but I keep breaking them. And so do you. Have you ever lied before? If you said no, that's at least your second lie. Men, have you ever looked at a woman lustfully? No? Me either. (BTW that's a lie!) Jesus says looking at a woman lustfully is as if we've committed adultery.

Ladies, have you ever had a girlfriend who got the guy, the outfit, the handbag, or another "thing" you just had to have? And no matter how hard you tried, you just couldn't be happy for her. If you are honest, maybe you kind of resented her for having it. That's called coveting! Like an X-ray, the Commandments reveal something is broken on the inside of all of us. Our very nature has been impacted by sin, and the diagnosis is not good. We are terminal.

I'm occasionally asked to speak at other churches or men's events. One particular church asked if I had a highlight reel from my playing days. This request got me wondering whether there was any footage I could grab from the internet. I immediately went to the Philadelphia Flyers website. Believe it or not, there was a link that said, *"Adam Burt's Highlights."* I'm not gonna lie, I had visions of me scoring a goal or possibly laying a crunching body check on someone. I pressed the link. It took me to a video clip of Tie Domi (Yes, that's his name) and another member of the Toronto Maple Leafs absolutely kicking the trash out of me! What! Wait! That can't be my HIGHLIGHT! C'mon man!

Unfortunately, that's your highlight too. The Apostle Paul sums it up like this:

None is righteous, no, not one; no one understands; no one seeks for God. All have turned aside; together they have become worthless; no one does good, not even one. Their throat is an open grave; they use their tongues to deceive. The venom of asps is under their lips. Their mouth is full of curses and bitterness. Their feet are swift to shed blood; in their paths are ruin and misery, and the way of peace they have not known. There is no fear of God before their eyes. (Romans 3:10-18 ESV)

And just in case you don't believe he's talking about you, he adds:

". . . for all have sinned and fall short of the glory of God." (Romans 3:23 ESV)

I know what you're thinking: I'm not perfect, but I'm not as bad as (you fill in the blank). The problem with that line of thinking is that God won't be judging you against other people. You will be judged against the holiness of God. In fact Jesus Himself, during His Sermon on the Mount, said:

"You therefore must be perfect, as your heavenly Father is perfect." (Matthew 5:48 ESV)

I think somewhere along the line, many of us bought into the idea that on the day of judgment, we will stand before God and he will operate these giant scales. If your good deeds outweigh your bad deeds, you will get into heaven. There are only two things wrong with that type of thinking:

#1 It's nowhere in the Bible.
#2 The Bible actually says our "good works" are like filthy rags before a Holy God.

All of us have become like one who is unclean, and all our righteous acts are like filthy rags." (Isaiah 64:6 NIV)

We have nothing to put on the good side of the scale. There nothing we can do to save ourselves. Our situation feels impossible. *"What's wrong with the world?"* Sin. It has messed up the world and us along with it. But there is Good News, God has a solution.

A HERO IS COMING

We all love a good hero story. In fact, according to Wikipedia, the Marvel Cinematic Universe ranks as the highest-grossing film series of all time, grossing over $29.8 billion. *Avengers* has the best average at nearly $1.9 billion per film. [3] The human heart loves a hero story.

Whether you realize it or not, the Marvel franchise of movies has trained all of us to actually sit and stay for the movie credits. You know, the boring section at the end of the film we really don't care about (sorry if that's harsh, but it's true). We patiently sit through it. Why? Because Marvel has trained us. After the credits, comes a new trailer. We get a glimpse of the next hero to come.

In Genesis, God takes a page out of the Marvel Comic's playbook. After Adam and Eve sin and the credits roll, we get a glimpse, a hint of a hero that would one day come. God speaks to the Serpent about a Serpent Crusher that would one day come:

> *And I will put enmity between you and the woman, and between your offspring and hers; he will crush your head, and you will strike his heel. (Genesis 3:15 NIV)*

I realize this chapter has been a bit of a downer and maybe more than a little hard to hear. Perhaps it has even left you a bit hopeless. Be encouraged. A hero is coming to the rescue. Remember how we felt at the end of *The Avengers: Infinity War*? If you recall, the evil Thanos captured all of the infinity stones. The bad guys just kept winning. Thanos snaps his fingers and many of our heroes fade away into thin air, and then the credits roll! Wait! What?! It can't end like that! In our guts, we know it can't end like that. And it doesn't. Wait for it. Be patient. *Avengers: Endgame* is coming. Our heroes will be reborn and evil will be forever destroyed. Does that story sound familiar to you? It should, because it's our story. *What's wrong with the world?* Sin. But good news! The Serpent Crusher is coming. Our Hero, the Savior of the world, is coming to rescue us from sin and the Serpent.

CHAPTER 4

"HOW CAN IT BE FIXED?" (THE CROSS/THE GOSPEL)

The reason the Son of God appeared was to destroy the works of the devil. (1 John 3:8 ESV)

What are you afraid of? Do you have any fears or phobias? Are you scared of heights? Snakes or maybe spiders? Is there something that strikes terror inside of you? If you ask any NHL player what his deepest, darkest fear is, his reply will be, "Skating past Bob Probert and my gloves accidentally fall off!" For those of you unfamiliar with Bob Probert, he is unanimously considered the toughest guy ever to play in the National Hockey League. The six-foot, three-inch winger amassed over three thousand penalty minutes during his NHL career. His face was usually marred with stitches or a black eye, which made him look that much more terrifying. All of his front teeth were missing, and it wasn't from poor dental hygiene. He was a fighter and had all the scars to prove it.

On December 14, 2001, Bob Probert and the Chicago Blackhawks were in town to take on the Atlanta Thrashers. I had signed with Atlanta as a free agent back in 2000, but would only play in twenty-seven games due to multiple back surgeries. (For the record, you know you're old when two of your former hockey teams no longer exist: the Hartford Whalers and Atlanta Thrashers.)

Our squad was a struggling expansion team just trying to figure things out. We added a young rookie to our club named Darcy Hordichuk. He was a great kid: charismatic, kind-hearted with a great sense of humor. But, when he stepped onto the ice, this six-foot, one-inch kid became something entirely different. He was a warrior and absolutely fearless.

The Blackhawks were dominating every aspect of this particular game. The scoreboard and all the momentum were tilted in Chicago's favor. The home crowd turned on us and grew increasingly more and more frustrated. The "boos" grew louder and louder. Our team was losing its will to compete. Something had to change. And it did! One young man decided, "Enough!" That man was Darcy Hordichuk.

There was only one way to recapture the crowd and the momentum—challenge Bob Probert to a fight. Your tough guy against our tough guy. Darcy dropped the gloves, and Probert gladly obliged and followed suit. The two squared off at center ice. This truly looked like a David and Goliath situation. Probert just appeared so much bigger and more menacing. It went REALLY BAD, REALLY FAST for Darcy. Probert seemed to land blow after blow. All hope for victory seemed to be lost.

Until Darcy somehow summoned the strength to deliver one more blow. He reached back and landed a bomb! A massive right-hand that buckled the giant! There was an audible gasp from the crowd. Our entire team rose to their feet. The momentum was shifting. With each blow Darcy landed, the crowd thundered in applause and cheers. The roar of the crowd swung back in our favor. He was winning! You could feel a tangible shift in the atmosphere. His courage was contagious. Everything changed, because one man decided, "Enough!"

In large part, that's our story. The human story. One man, the promised "Serpent Crusher," would arrive on the scene and declare, "Enough!" And with his life, death, burial, and resurrection, there was a cosmic shift in God's creation. Everything would change.

ON THE CLOCK

"Therefore, rejoice, O heavens and you who dwell in them! But woe to you, O earth and sea, for the devil has come down to you in great wrath, because he knows that his time is short!"
(Revelation 12:12 ESV)

Satan knows *his time is short*. God promised a hero would come, "the seed of the woman" would crush the Serpent's head. Apparently, God's idea of "a short time" is very different from ours. Humanity would wait for thousands of years for their hero to arrive. How he arrived will take a bit of explaining.

Researchers today estimate the average attention span of an American is roughly eight seconds long, slightly more than that of a goldfish. I believe you're an overachiever and can follow along as we arrive at the Serpent Crusher. Buckle up. I'm about to take you through thousands of years of human history in a few paragraphs:

Adam and Eve are kicked out of the Garden of Eden. Their son Cain kills Abel. Humanity's sin increases, and the world continues its downward spiral. God decides to flood the earth and start over. One man, Noah, finds favor with God. He and his family jump onto the ark and are spared from the flood. Afterwards, God's commandment to Noah is nearly identical to the one he gave to Adam and Eve:

And God blessed Noah and his sons and said to them, "Be fruitful and multiply and fill the earth." (Genesis 9:1 ESV)

Unfortunately, it only takes a chapter or two after the flood for man to once again grow sinful. In Genesis 12, God makes a covenant with a man named Abram. We would later know him as Abraham, and God said to him:

"And I will make of you a great nation, and I will bless you and make your name great, so that you will be a blessing. I will bless those who bless you, and him who dishonors you I will curse, and in you all the families of the earth shall be blessed."
(Genesis 12:2-3 ESV)

Through Abraham's seed God was going to bless the world. Abraham had Isaac. Isaac had twin boys: Jacob and Esau. Jacob took two wives (never a good idea). The two wives vie for Jacob's affections by seeing who can bear the most children. If this were a reality TV show, it would definitely be called *Baby Wars*. Jacob has twelve sons. These twelve sons will become the twelve tribes of Israel. Eventually, the family settles in Egypt. One son is critical to our story: Judah.

"Judah is a lion's cub; from the prey, my son, you have gone up. He stooped down; he crouched as a lion and as a lioness; who dares rouse him? The scepter shall not depart from Judah, nor the ruler's staff from between his feet, until tribute comes to him; and to him shall be the obedience of the peoples." (Genesis 49:9-10 ESV)

A Lion from the Tribe of Judah. Does that sound familiar? A ruler shall arise from the line of Judah. But in the meantime, Pharaoh later enslaves the twelve tribes of Israel. God raises up a deliverer named Moses. (You know you're a big deal when people refer to you by one name: Oprah, Jordan, Prince . . . Moses!) He leads God's people out of Egypt, and Joshua takes them into the Promised Land. Israel becomes a nation with a line of rulers, both good and bad. One king is named David, He kills a really tall guy named Goliath and establishes Israel as a superpower. At the end of his life, God speaks to David:

> *"When your days are fulfilled and you lie down with your fathers, I will raise up your offspring after you, who shall come from your body, and I will establish his kingdom . . . And your house and your kingdom shall be made sure forever before me. Your throne shall be established forever." (2 Samuel 7:12-16 ESV)*

God promises that through David's line, He would raise up a King whose Kingdom would never end. David was a Giant Slayer but his progeny would be a Serpent Crusher. David's son Solomon becomes king. He was known as the wisest man that ever lived. I'm not sure that's true. He had seven hundred wives. Not a wise move. Unfortunately, Solomon's son was such a poor leader that civil war broke out, and the Kingdom was split in two, Israel to the North and Judah to the south. Eventually, both kingdoms were overrun and many of God's people were taken captive. While in captivity, a prophet named Daniel (You may remember Daniel and the Lions den?) prophesied of a hero to come:

> *"I saw in the night visions, and behold, with the clouds of heaven there came one like a son of man, and he came to the Ancient of Days and was presented before him. And to him was given dominion and glory and a kingdom, that all peoples, nations, and languages should serve him; his dominion is an everlasting dominion, which shall not pass away, and his kingdom one that shall not be destroyed." (Daniel 7:13-14 ESV)*

A "Son of Man" would come with power and dominion to establish an everlasting Kingdom. It's a prophetic whisper, a hint of the Serpent Crusher who is to come.

The Old Testament prophets continue to beat this drum over and over again: "He's coming, He's coming, He's coming."

Finally we get to the last book of the Old Testament, the book of Malachi, in which the Lord declares through the Prophet Malachi:

> *"But for you who fear my name, the sun of righteousness shall rise with healing in its wings. You shall go out leaping like calves from the stall. And you shall tread down the wicked, for they will be ashes under the soles of your feet, on the day when I act, says the LORD of hosts." (Malachi 4:2-3 ESV)*

A "sun of righteousness" would one day appear. Our enemies would be destroyed and "healing" would be in his wings. It is the final promise of a coming hero.

The last page of your Old Testament to the first page of your New Testament represents four-hundred years of human history, four centuries of prophetic SILENCE. Deafening silence. No words from God. No more promises of a coming hero.

Did God's promise fail? Was the "seed of the woman" somehow stopped?

Finally, the silence was broken with the scream of a baby born in Bethlehem. With that child's first cry, the night sky cracked open, followed by the thunderous declaration from the angelic heavenly hosts:

> *And the angel said to them, "Fear not, for behold, I bring you good news of great joy that will be for all the people. For unto you is born this day in the city of David a Savior, who is Christ the Lord." (Luke 2:10-11 ESV)*

And with the birth of that baby came the hope of mankind and the shudder of hell. Merry Christmas! The long-awaited Serpent Crusher had finally arrived. Immanuel, God with us. Satan knows his time is short.

THE GOSPEL: THE GREAT EXCHANGE

For our sake he [God] made him [Jesus] to be sin who knew no sin, so that in him we might become the righteousness of God. (2 Corinthians 5:21 ESV)

There are certain iconic moments in history that time stamp our lives. Things like 9/11, the tragic death of Kobe Bryant, or the OJ verdict. These moments just seem to be screen shots taken by our minds that stay with us forever. We remember where we were and what we were doing.

March 6, 1999, do you remember where you were and what you were doing? You should. This was the unforgettable moment in our nation's history when all-star NHL defenseman Adam Burt (me) was traded from the Carolina Hurricanes to the Philadelphia Flyers for forward Andrei Kovalenko. There was an exchange of one player for another. (By the way, none of that all-star stuff is true—but it's my book so get off of me!)

Some two thousand years ago, there was another trade. Theologians call it "the Great Exchange." One man, Jesus, was given over in exchange for the sins of the world. God poured His wrath for our sins—past, present and future—onto Jesus. We in exchange received the perfect righteousness of Christ. A truly "Great Exchange." It is "the Gospel" or "Good News." I believe it's the best news possible! As Paul writes to the Romans:

> *For I am not ashamed of the gospel, for it is the power of God for salvation to everyone who believes. (Romans 1:16 ESV)*

How can what's wrong be made right? By the perfect life and sacrificial death of Jesus, the Serpent Crusher. Through the cross, our sins are forgiven and we are reconciled back to God. In Christ, both *SALVATION* and *RESTORATION* become possible.

SALVATION AND THE PROBLEM OF SIN

Do you think a car can have a demon? Theologically, I don't believe it's possible. But if it were, my 2010 Acura MDX definitely had one! I was hit in that car five times. If it wasn't a demon, it was some kind of cosmic curse. I had been to the local body shop so many times they knew me by name.

The fourth time I was hit, a young girl just learning to drive T-boned my car. I felt bad for her, but c'mon, man! My car limped back to the body shop. I was cordially greeted by the appraiser, "Welcome back, Mr. Burt," as if I were returning to my favorite local restaurant or drinking establishment. After a few weeks, the car was repaired and I was back on the road again.

One evening I had to pick up a few pastors from Laguardia Airport and drop them off in Manhattan. I picked them up in my newly repaired ride and made my way back into the City. Trying to maneuver in Manhattan can be treacherous. Cabs, cars, bikes, and buses are coming at you from all directions. I arrived safely at the first pastor's street corner and stopped. He thanked me for the ride and then proceeded to open the rear door… into oncoming traffic!! With its horn blaring, a cab hit the rear door and literally wrapped it around to the front of my car! Traffic slowed, drivers yelled and honked as I jumped out of the car in disbelief. Have you ever been so angry that you can't even fake being polite? I turned around and said, "Bro, get out of my car and go home!" I managed to bend the door back into place so I could drive home. The following morning, I made my way back to the body shop. "Welcome back, Mr. Burt." Five grand was the estimate to repair the damage!

Several days later, I met up with the perpetrating pastor. He apologized again and again and finally asked, "What can I do to make it right?" "What can you do to make it right? You can give me five grand!" I said. "I don't have five grand," he replied. "Well then, I guess there is *nothing* you can do to make it right." But you see, *somebody has to pay to fix it!* And that is the problem with sin. Someone has to pay to fix it.

JESUS PAYS THE BILL

For the wages of sin is death, but the free gift of God is eternal life in Christ Jesus our Lord. (Romans 6:23)

I'll often hear people ask, *"Why can't God just forgive sin? Why the gruesome brutality of the cross?"* God does forgive sin, but He can't *JUST* forgive sin. Sin must be paid for or else God would be unjust. We want a God of justice sitting on the throne of the universe. An unjust judge would be untenable.

Imagine the outrage if Larry Nassar, the convicted pedophile that sexually assaulted some 265 little girls, were just randomly set free by a judge. The judge bangs the gavel and flippantly declares, *"I forgive you."* We would burn that courtroom to the ground. Why? Because it's unjust!

We love justice. I don't think it's even debatable. The last time I checked, there were roughly seventy courtroom TV shows: *Divorce Court, People's Court, Judge Judy, Judge Wapner, Judge Brown*, not to mention all the legal dramas like *Law and Order, L.A. Law*, and *Matlock*. The list goes on and on.

We can't get enough justice. It's been hardwired into our DNA. I'll prove it to you. Have you ever been watching a movie and the villain is wicked? I mean really awful. At the end of the movie, that guy has to die badly, doesn't he? And if he doesn't, don't you feel a bit unsatisfied? Unfulfilled? That's your inner sense of justice at work. But herein lies the problem: When we are sinned against, we want justice. When we sin against others, you know what we want? Mercy and forgiveness. What is God to do? He's holy and must do justice, but He's also loving and wants to forgive. What's the answer? The cross of Christ! It's at the cross that justice and mercy meet. Jesus absorbs the righteous wrath of God for us on the cross (Justice). He dies, so that you and I may live (mercy). As Paul writes:

God shows his love for us in that while we were still sinners, Christ died for us. Since, therefore, we have now been justified by his blood, much more shall we be saved by him from the wrath of God. (Romans 5:8-9 ESV)

September 29, 2006, Ramadi, Iraq. Seal Team Three was deployed to help train Iraqi soldiers. Delta Platoon was stationed atop a local building to ward off insurgents and keep an eye out for any rebel activity. The mood was very business-like and quiet as each Seal Team member went about his duties. The quiet was broken with a loud cry, "GRENADE!" Without hesitation, Seal Michael Monsoor jumped on top of the live grenade moments before detonating. The deadly blast was absorbed by the brave soldier. He died so that the entire team could be saved. [1] One of the Seal Team survivors was quoted as saying, "Mikey looked death in the face and said, 'You cannot take my brothers. I will go in their stead.'" [2]

Michael's remains were returned stateside to be laid to rest. What came next was so incredibly powerful. As the wooden casket made its way to the burial site, Seal Team members dressed in full uniform were arrayed on either side of the casket. As the casket passed by, each Seal Team member removed their gold Trident pin and placed it on top of the casket. One Seal after another laid down their prized pin as a sign of unity. It was a declaration, *"What Michael stands for, we stand for!"*

When the coffin arrived at its final resting spot, it was completely covered in gold Trident pins.

Michael absorbed death on behalf of his brothers so that they might live. Jesus did the same for us. In dying, Jesus absorbed death on our behalf and in rising from the dead, Jesus declared the *"death of death!"* He's not saying that we won't ever die. He's saying, we are safe in dying. Because He rose from the dead, we can be confident that we too will one day rise from the dead. Now death is simply the door to resurrection and eternal life. Until that day, we align our lives with our

Hero. Seal Team members laid down their Trident pins in agreement. We lay down our lives in agreement with Christ. What HE stands for, we stand for. Which brings us to Restoration.

FROM SALVATION TO RESTORATION:

"For He must remain in heaven until the time for the final restoration of all things." (Acts 3:21 NLT)

There is something about the bond between a father and a son. Jimmie Bradford and his son Taylor had such a bond. They both loved cars. In particular, they loved a beige 1979 Lincoln Continental the size of a small ocean liner. The two men laughed and reminisced as they washed the enormous car together. Taylor received a scholarship to play football at the University of Memphis, and as a parting gift, his father gave him the keys to the Lincoln.

Fast-forward several months, tragically and senselessly, Taylor was gunned down while driving in the '79 Lincoln. The car was destroyed as it veered off the road, violently smashing into a tree. Jimmie Bradford received a call that no father should ever receive. His son was dead.

The grieving father drove to Memphis and towed his deceased son's decimated car back home. Jimmie often walked around the car, talking to his son as if he were still alive. Several times a month, he'd wash the mangled vehicle and talk to his boy. It was his way of clinging to the memory of his son.

Sometime later, several hundred miles away, a Wisconsin auto body shop owner, Jim Harris, caught wind of the tragic story on A&E. Harris couldn't shake the haunting image of Jimmie Bradford washing his son's wrecked car. He had this thought: *"I can fix it. I can fix that car and make it brand-new again."* [3]

After several attempts to track down the Bradfords, Harris finally succeeded and awkwardly asked if they'd allow a stranger, from hundreds of miles away, to repair their precious son's car. Surprisingly, they agreed.

One year later, Jim Harris returned the car back to the Bradfords. Free of charge. Fully restored. Like brand-new. They not only received the car back, but in a strange way, they got a piece of their son back.

Restoration. Our hearts long for it. Sin and Satan have destroyed God's good creation. Jesus, just like Jim Harris, sees the devastation and declares, *"I can fix it. I can make it brand-new again."* In Revelation we read of Jesus,

> *And He who was seated on the throne said, "Behold, I am making all things new." (Revelation 21:5 ESV)*

Deep down inside, all of us can feel the clock ticking. Time as we know it is finite and will one day come to an end. We read about it in novels and see it in Hollywood films. "The Apocalypse," "Armageddon," the "Last Days"—whatever you want to call it. Time and space will come to a crescendo and there will be this epic battle between good and evil. The Bible, however, describes this epic battle a bit differently. It's actually kind of anticlimactic:

> *And then the lawless one will be revealed, whom the Lord Jesus will overthrow with the breath of his mouth and destroy by the splendor of his coming. (2 Thessalonians 2:8 NIV)*

At the end of time, there will be no epic struggle. Jesus will say, "ENOUGH!" He will exhale and destroy his enemies. You see, at the cross, Jesus destroyed sin's POWER. At the end of time, Jesus will remove sins PRESENCE. The Serpent will be cast into the eternal lake of fire, and Jesus will make *"all things new."*

Restoration. On that day, the Lord will once again knit heaven and earth together as He did in the Garden of Eden. Perfect beauty and Shalom will be restored.

If you've traveled at all, you know there are some truly breathtaking places on our planet. The beautiful blue-green of the Caribbean. The sun setting in the Florida Keys. The awe-inspiring views from the Grand Canyon or the vast array of colors in the Northeast as the leaves change from summer to fall. These wonders are soul stirring to experience, and yet, not all is as it should be. God's creation is currently under a curse due to sin. But one day, we will see it restored and renewed. One early church father, St. Augustine, said it this way: *"If these be the beauties afforded to sinful man, what does God have in store for those who love Him?"* [4] The answer to this question is restoration, the world as it should be.

All of us have experienced pain and suffering in this broken world, some more than others. The promise of restoration holds true for you as well. In the end, somehow, someway God will remove our pain and sorrow:

> *"He will wipe away every tear from their eyes, and death shall be no more, neither shall there be mourning, nor crying, nor pain anymore, for the former things have passed away."*
> *(Revelation 21:4 ESV)*

I once heard the late pastor and theologian Tim Keller describe the concept of *sad things becoming untrue*. Keller recounts a horrific nightmare. His entire family was brutally murdered. The dream was so vivid and real that when he awoke, it took a few moments for reality to come back into focus. Once it did, he realized his wife and children were still very much alive. Joy, gratitude, and affection flooded his heart! For him, sad things had become untrue. [5] And that is our ultimate reality. God will take all the pain, suffering, and sorrow we've endured in *this life* and somehow make it untrue in the *next life*. All you've endured here, will multiply your joy there.

But until that time, God has made you an agent of restoration here on earth.

AGENTS OF RESTORATION:

They shall build up the ancient ruins; they shall raise up the former devastations; they shall repair the ruined cities, the devastations of many generations. (Isaiah 61:4 ESV)

Have you ever ridden a New York City subway? It really is a fascinating experience. I remember traveling with my eleven-year-old daughter. The subway car was packed, standing room only. My daughter and I stood as the car raced down the tracks. I was relishing this daddy-daughter moment. My "baby girl" was clinging to my arm affectionately, or so I thought. She would later tell me she just didn't want to touch anything on those filthy subway cars. My arm was the cleanest option! Oh well, I'll take it however I can get it.

At one of the subway stops, three grown men boarded the car. As the doors shut, the men announced, "Good afternoon, everyone!" With those words, every New Yorker has been trained: Put your head down and stare at the floor because people are about to ask you for money!

As everyone stared at the floor, the three men moved to the front of the car and announced, "We aren't here to ask you for anything. We simply want to lift your spirits and bless you with a song about our Savior." The trio immediately burst into an old familiar hymn. With each chorus, something bizarre happened.

Heads started lifting and hands started clapping. One by one each reluctant passenger was won over by song. Eventually, the entire subway car was thundering away in praise. Somehow a worship service had broken out. I seriously wondered if someone was punking me. Was this really happening?

The subway car slowed to its next stop, and the three gentlemen exited with these words, "GOD BLESS YOU!" The doors closed. The car sped away and immediately, everyone went back to staring at the floor in complete and utter silence.

What just took place? Then it struck me, those men had been RESTORED in order to help RESTORE. Those three men were made new and now sought to bring renewal to others. Wherever you go and whatever you do, do it in such a way as to glorify God and bless the world. Those men decided to be a *thermostat* instead of a *thermometer*. They decided to set the spiritual temperature rather than simply <u>take</u> it. How can the world be fixed? By being a spiritual thermostat and setting the spiritual temperature wherever you go and whatever you do. You can be an agent of restoration. You can restore a little piece of Eden. Jesus says it like this:

> "<u>You are the salt of the earth</u>, *but if salt has lost its taste, how shall its saltiness be restored? It is no longer good for anything except to be thrown out and trampled under people's feet. You are the light of the world. A city set on a hill cannot be hidden."*
> *(Matthew 5:13-14 ESV)*

How can what's broken be fixed? By you being the salt of the earth and the light of the world. By you not just making a living, but making a difference. You have been RESTORED back to God in order to become an agent of RESTORATION.

When you become aware of all Jesus has done for you in the cross, it becomes nearly impossible to simply sit on the sidelines and do nothing. Gratitude compels us to get involved, to partner with God as agents of restoration. We push back all that's dark and broken in the world. That push is our ultimate expression of gratitude. It's how we say "Thank You" for all He's done.

I'll end this section with the story of Eddie Rickenbacker. Eddie seemed to be a rather odd old man. He was seen regularly walking up and down the ocean pier with a pail full of raw shrimp. He randomly tossed shrimp into the sky out over the water. Seagulls gathered for the feast. They dive-bombed and scooped up the delicious morsels before they hit the water. With each handful of shrimp, the old man was heard whispering, "Thank you, thank you."

The backstory: Eddie Rickenbacker is the most decorated pilot in World War I history. It was during World War II, however, that Eddie and his crew were shot down over the Pacific Ocean.

He and his seven crew members survived the plane's plunge into the Pacific and made it safely to the emergency life rafts. Lost at sea for over a week, the crew's food rations were exhausted and so were they. They needed a miracle.

Eddie led the group in a time of prayer and then decided they should all try and rest to conserve energy. As Eddie lay back on the life raft, attempting to get some sleep, he felt something land on his head. It was a seagull. Eddie lay motionless, not wanting to startle the bird. The crew was frozen as they watched in disbelief. Eddie waited for the perfect moment to strike. Suddenly, like a bolt of lightning, Eddie snatched hold of the bird. Feathers flew into the air, as Eddie and the crew ripped into the bird's raw carcass. It wasn't much of a meal for the starving group, but the entrails were used as bait to fish. Their catch of fish was more than enough to sustain them at sea. Eventually, they were found, rescued, and brought back to the United States.

Now, like clockwork, Eddie Rickenbacker returns to the ocean pier to pay homage to one bird's sacrifice. He returns with shrimp in hand to say, "Thank you. Thank you." [6]

I can't help but think, that's how we should all live. In light of the sacrifice of God's own Son on our behalf, we should live our life in constant thanksgiving and gratitude.

He died for everyone so that those who receive his new life will no longer live for themselves. Instead, they will live for Christ, who died and was raised for them. (2 Corinthians 5:15 NLT)

In the marketplace of ideas, I believe Christianity answers life's biggest questions best. I pray that you will come to the same conclusion. I want you to win in the game of life. But in the end, you have to decide for yourself who you will play for:

"And if it is evil in your eyes to serve the LORD, choose this day whom you will serve, whether the gods your fathers served in the region beyond the River, or the gods of the Amorites in whose land you dwell. But as for me and my house, we will serve the LORD."
(Joshua 24:15 ESV)

"BEFORE YOU MOVE ON"

On January 15, 2009, US Airways flight 1549 departed from LaGuardia airport en route to Charlotte, North Carolina. Moments into the flight, something went terribly wrong. As the plane ascended, several birds struck the engines, disabling them. Captain Chesley "Sully" Sullenberger was forced to make a life-or-death decision in a matter of seconds. Does he attempt to turn the plane around and return to LaGuardia airport without the use of his engines?

Or, does he land the plane on the Hudson River? Captain Sully chooses the latter. It became known as "the Miracle on the Hudson."

Passenger Ric Elias describes how eerie it is to be on an aircraft and not hear the hum of the engines. The silence screamed, "Something is wrong!" Just when it seemed the situation couldn't get any worse, the silence was broken by these words from the cockpit: *"Brace for IMPACT!"* For Ric Elias, those words were very clarifying. In that kind of moment, the fog of misplaced priorities lifts. What's important and what's not important becomes crystal clear. [7]

This is your *"brace for impact"* moment. It's estimated, you will make roughly 35,000 decisions today. What will I eat? What will I wear? What will I say? Some decisions are bigger than others. One decision stands out above them all: *"What will I do with Jesus?"* Will you bow your knee to Him as your Savior and Lord? Or, will you simply dismiss Him as a good man who was tragically killed on a cross? You must decide. You must "brace for impact."

Would you like to have a relationship with Jesus? Would you like to be confident where you will spend eternity? You can be! It's as easy as "ABC."

A= **ADMIT** you are a sinner in need of a Savior.

B= **BELIEVE** that Jesus lived the perfect life on your behalf and died on the cross for your sins.

C= **CONFESS** Jesus as your Lord and Savior.

If you confess with your mouth that Jesus is Lord and believe in your heart that God raised him from the dead, you will be saved. (Romans 10:9 ESV)

SECTION 2

"TRAINING TO WIN"

Train yourself for godliness; for while bodily training is of some value, godliness is of value in every way, as it holds promise for the present life and also for the life to come. (1 Timothy 4:7-8)

It's still regarded as the greatest moment in our country's sporting history: the Men's US Olympic Hockey Team's 1980 win. At that time, our country was floundering with a failing economy, inflation, division, and political unrest. Sound familiar? Yet, one team would galvanize the nation. One miraculous moment would make us forget all of it. The chants of *"USA"* could be heard on every street corner. Hall of Fame broadcaster Al Michaels challenged us to believe again when he announced, *"Do you believe in Miracles?"* And suddenly, we did!

If you recall, the United States and Russia were in the thick of the Cold War. The Soviets were dominating the Olympic landscape. There were no such things as "Dream Teams." Pro athletes were ineligible for competition, and the Soviets had their way. Iconic US team coach Herb Brooks was left with the impossible task of transforming a bunch of amateur collegiate athletes into a team for the ages. How would he do it you ask? *Training.* Again and again. Over and over. *Training.* Brooks was relentless as he pushed these young men to the breaking point. Little did they know, on the other side of training was a "Miracle on Ice."

We see this story powerfully captured in the 2004 film *Miracle*. Kurt Russell masterfully stars as Coach Herb Brooks. His frustration mounts as he watches his team play like a bunch of individuals. Brooks, aware of what it will take to beat the Soviets, challenges his players, "This cannot be a team of COMMON men. Common men do nothing. YOU must be a group of UNCOMMON men." And with that, he starts grinding these young men down. He skates them back and forth, up and down the ice. Before they can stop and catch their breath, Brooks barks out, *"Again!"* and sends the exhausted players back down the ice.

Periodically, he'd pause, single out a player, and snarl, "Who do you play for?" Inevitably, the player would give his collegiate team's name. Wrong answer! Brooks would send the team back down the ice. *"Again!"* As the players gasp for air, Captain Mike Eruzione yells out unexpectedly, "Mike Eruzione from Winthrop, Massachusetts." Brooks, somewhat startled, responds with a curious tone to his voice, "Who do you play for?"

"I play for . . ." Eruzione pauses as he fights for breath. "I play for THE UNITED STATES OF AMERICA!" Satisfied, Coach Brooks responds, "That's all, gentleman!" [1] Something shifted from that moment forward. Something changed. This group of individuals became a team. *Training* united both the team and the nation. *Training* is the process that makes miracles possible. Do you believe in miracles?

> **Now when they saw the boldness of Peter and John, and perceived that they were uneducated, common men, they were astonished. And they recognized that they had been with Jesus.**
> **(Acts 4:13 ESV)**

Jesus trained twelve common men, and they became uncommon. These uncommon men "turned the world upside down" (Acts 17:6). If you want to win in the Christian life, training is a nonnegotiable. The Apostle Paul puts it this way:

I discipline my body like an athlete, training it to do what it should. Otherwise, I fear that after preaching to others I myself might be disqualified. (1 Corinthians 9:27 NLT)

In order to become uncommon players in the game of life we need TRAINING. In section 2 we will discuss four training nonnegotiables required to win in the Christian life. First, we need the "Game Plan" or the Bible which we'll explore in chapter 5. In Chapter 6 we'll discuss "Talking with the Great One," through prayer. Chapter 7 delves into our source of Power, which comes from "The Holy Spirit." Finally, chapter 8 looks at "the Church" our spiritual teammates.

CHAPTER 5

"GAME PLAN" (THE BIBLE)

All Scripture is breathed out by God and profitable for teaching, for reproof, for correction, and for training in righteousness, that the man of God may be complete, equipped for every good work.
(2 Timothy 3:16-17 ESV)

If you've ever seen films like, *Any Given Sunday, Remember the Titans,* or the aforementioned movie *Miracle,* there is always an iconic "pump up speech" scene. The locker room is dead silent as the coach paces back and forth. The players track the coach's every movement. Slowly and deliberately he maneuvers as the players anxiously await their orders. The coach has a rolled-up copy of the lineup in his hand. He raises it like a sword to the sky, and then points it at each one of his athletes. The speech that follows would put Churchill or William Wallace to shame. The players rise from the locker room benches, inspired, transformed. The euphoric team pours onto the court, field, or rink and shocks the world. That's usually how it goes in the movies, but rarely, if ever, does it play out like that in real life. I've spent a lot of time in locker rooms and have yet to hear that speech. Actually, they've all been rather anticlimactic and at times somewhat comical.

My first year as a pro, our head coach was a man named Jack "Tex" Evans. He was nominated for Coach of the Year the previous season. As a new player, I was so excited to hear his first "pump up speech." Anticipating something inspiring, I watched and listened as Jack walked through the locker room, and, in the most monotone voice imaginable, mumbled, "Let's go, boys." As he walked out of the room and into the arena, I remember thinking, "That's it?! That's the pump up speech?"

During my final season in the NHL, I had a coach that swore every other word. He was a great guy, but had a horrible mouth. His favorite word by far was the "F-bomb," and he managed to use it as an adjective, adverb, verb, noun, and proper noun. It was truly impressive. After one pump up speech, I turned and looked at our team's captain, Ray Ferraro. He simply looked back at me and said, "Twenty-three". "What do you mean twenty-three?" I asked. "Twenty-three F-bombs," he replied. We cracked up and promptly proceeded to take to the ice and lose another hockey game. So much for the pump up speech.

My coach's speeches were memorable for all the wrong reasons. Jesus, however, gives one of the most memorable monologues ever recorded in Matthew 5–7. It's known as the "Sermon on the Mount." It covers all of life's bases: how to pray, how to use money, morality, the "Golden Rule," how not to worry or judge others. Jesus ends this historic speech with the big takeaway:

"Everyone then who hears these words of mine and does them will be like a wise man who built his house on the rock. And the rain fell, and the floods came, and the winds blew and beat on that house, but it did not fall, because it had been founded on the rock. And everyone who hears these words of mine and does not do them will be like a foolish man who built his house on the sand. And the rain fell, and the floods came, and the winds blew and beat against

that house, and it fell, and great was the fall of it."
(Matthew 7:24-27 ESV)

Jesus says by hearing and following the Word of God (the Bible), you are literally storm proofing your life. Notice, storms come for ALL of us. However, those who hear and do the words of Jesus are building their life on the rock. Whatever life may throw at you, you won't be shaken if your life is built on the firm foundation of God's Word. Conversely, if you disregard Jesus' words, it's only a matter of time until the storms of life come. Your life built on sand will not withstand the onslaught of life's storms. Have you "storm-proofed" your life?

It was October of 2018. Hurricane Michael, a category 5 hurricane, ripped through the Florida panhandle to the tune of over eight billion dollars worth of damage. Michael literally leveled everything in its path—or almost everything. One home remained standing. It was owned by Dr. LeBron Lackey, who designed the house with one question in mind: "What would survive the 'Big One'?" Every aspect of the home was built above code. He named the house, "The Sand Palace." [1] He should have called it "The Rock." Is your life built on the Rock of God's Word, or have ignored the hard questions, cut corners, and built on sand?

THE BIBLE

The term "Bible" comes from the Greek word "biblia" which simply means "books." The Bible is made up of sixty-six books and broken up into two sections, the Old and New Testaments. The Old Testament has thirty-nine books and the New Testament has twenty-seven. It was written over the course of 1,500 years, on three different continents (Africa, Asia, and Europe), in multiple languages (Hebrew, Greek, and Aramaic).

Forty different authors, ranging from kings to fishermen, contributed to the Bible, and yet, it tells one cohesive story, the story of God's rescue of humanity and the restoration of all things. The Bible is our game plan for winning in life.

Unfortunately, ignorance about the Bible is steadily increasing. Entertainer and proud critic of Christianity, Bill Maher, observes, *"To most Christians, the Bible is like a software license. Nobody actually reads it. They just scroll to the bottom and click 'I agree'."* [2] This commentary is sad but often true. Our biblical illiteracy is robbing us of the abundant life Jesus wants for us. The Prophet Hosea said:

> ***My people are destroyed for lack of knowledge.***
> ***(Hosea 4:6 ESV)***

I don't need to be a prophet in order to know a few things about you. If you're a Christian but fail to read your Bible on a regular basis, I know you are losing a lot in your life. I've never met a weak Christian who regularly reads the Word of God. Nor have I ever met a strong Christian who didn't read the Word. Reading the Bible is a nonnegotiable part of the winning Christian life. I want you to win.

I became a Christian around the age of eleven, but I didn't get serious about reading my Bible until about the age of sixteen. I remember feeling so insecure and unsure at that time in my life. I needed something to ground me, something timeless and true. The Bible became my "Game Plan" for living. I made a promise to myself and to the

Lord; I would read one chapter a day for the rest of my life. I can't begin to tell you how many days I read a chapter and had NO idea what I just read. Some chapters had these long genealogies that felt like reading a phone book. Others had confusing names or prophetic visions that just seemed weird. Yet, slowly and steadily, the story started to make sense. The fog started to lift, and the Gospel became increasingly more clear. It began to shape the way I viewed the world and how I lived. As the pieces fell into place, a newfound peace and security began forming inside me just through faithful reading. Then one day it struck me. The Bible is more than words written on a page. It is alive. When you place the Word of God at the center of your heart, it changes you from the inside out.

For the word of God is living and active, sharper than any two-edged sword, piercing to the division of soul and of spirit, of joints and of marrow, and discerning the thoughts and intentions of the heart. (Hebrews 4:12 ESV)

Philip Mauro was the "Forrest Gump" of his day. Just as Forrest Gump seemed to stumble into many of America's most iconic scenes, Vietnam, Watergate, the assassination of JFK. Philip Mauro, born in 1859, was involved in an amazing number of historical events. For starters, he was aboard the RMS Carpathia which rescued the survivors of the *Titanic*. He wrote the legal briefs for the "Scopes Monkey Trial" and shared his faith with Thomas Edison!

Mauro was an attorney, author, and follower of Jesus. He wrote an essay entitled "Life in the Word." In it, he argues that the Bible displays all the characteristics of being alive:

It has perennial freshness. It is non-obsolete and always contemporary. It is indestructible. It is a discerner, a "critic," of hearts and minds. It is remarkably translatable. It lodges in hearts and grows. It transforms other life. [3]

A PERENNIAL FRESHNESS

The Bible always has something new and fresh to say to us each day. As a hockey player, I carried my Bible with me on every road trip. It didn't matter if the team traveled by bus or by airplane, "The Book" was with me. My teammates were puzzled at the fact that I kept reading the same book over and over again. Finally, one player inquired, "Haven't you finished reading that book yet?" I cracked up and told him it doesn't work like that. The Bible is a book you never finish. In fact, I've been reading it for forty years, and it still has more to say. I learn something new every time I open it. It is always fresh.

NON-OBSOLETE AND ALWAYS CONTEMPORARY

The Bible is timeless Truth. Because it's Truth, it never changes or goes out of style. There is no "expiration date" on the Word of God.

My experience traveling in both the NHL and NFL is far different than my travel as a pastor. In pro sports it's all chartered airplanes, great food, first class seating with tons of space. My first flight as a pastor was very, very different. I had a middle seat squashed between two large men with a median weight of about 240 pounds! We were in the last row of the plane, so our seats wouldn't recline and the restrooms were right behind us. First world problems, I know. But, I recall praying and asking God to please kill me.

One particular flight stands out to me and illustrates God's timeless Truth. My wife and I were seated on the flight as the flight crew boarded the plane. You could tell they were running behind schedule as the stewardesses hurried about. The lead attendant was a young woman and one of her subordinates was old. I mean really old. She looked like someone's sweet grandmother and had the demeanor to match. She stopped and chatted with all the passengers as if she had all the time in the world. I could see the lead attendant getting increasingly agitated by how slow she was moving. After takeoff, the food and beverage service started. The old attendant was at the front of the plane with the drink cart taking orders and the younger attendant was near the back of the plane. The old attendant was caught up in a conversation with a passenger and didn't realize she forgot to apply the brake on the beverage cart. The cart went streaking down the aisle out of control. It struck the unsuspecting lead attendant right in the rear end! Startled and frustrated, she looked at me and burst out, "She just needs to retire!"

Oftentimes, that is the perspective people take with the Word of God. They believe it's just old and outdated. The Bible needs to retire or get with the times. Its teachings about morality and human behavior are stale. Take sex for example. The Bible teaches that sexual intimacy should exist between one man and one woman in the covenant of marriage. I can already see your eyes rolling and hear you thinking, "That's so old-school." It is old, like Adam and Eve old. But, what if it works? What if it's the way God designed His creation to flourish?

The 1960s brought us the sexual revolution. We were doing away with that "old-school" sex and marriage stuff. We had progressed beyond such archaic ideas. What did we get in exchange for "free" non-committal sex? We saw an increase in divorce and the devastation of the family unit. Women and children have suffered the most. Single moms have been given the task of raising their kids while working a full-time job to support the household. Children have been forced to grow up without a father in the home. Sex may have seemed free but it cost us so much. No matter how hard we have tried to get away from God's design for sex, we keep coming back to the Truth. God's Word works best.

The Huffington Post, by no means a Christian publication, recently wrote an article entitled, "Want More and Better Sex? Get Married and Stay Married." [4] The article highlights how married couples have more and better sex than singles.

The Washington Post, again not a Christian publication, highlighted an opinion piece entitled, "Consent Is Not Enough. We Need A New Sexual Ethic." [5] The author highlights how many people no longer feel safe during "hookups." Simply consenting to sex has left the experience hollow and empty. When asked what would make it better, the response boiled down to three things: listening, mutual responsibility and willing the good of the other. This sounds a lot like MARRIAGE! God's Word never grows old because it is timeless TRUTH.

IT IS INDESTRUCTIBLE

The Word of God is indestructible.

Yemelyan Yaroslavsky was a Russian politician, journalist, and outspoken atheist. He was quoted as saying, "Christianity is like a nail. The harder you strike it the deeper it goes." [6] The same can be said for the Bible. Opponents of the Bible have tried for millennia to dismiss its veracity. French philosopher Voltaire declared in 1776, "One hundred years from my day, there will not be a Bible in the earth except one that is looked upon by an antiquarian curiosity seeker." [7] One hundred years later, Voltaire was dead, and his own house and press were being used to print and store Bibles by the Geneva Bible Society.

Brilliant minds such as C. S. Lewis, Josh McDowell, and Lee Strobel went on a journey to debunk Christianity and the Bible. However, in their attempt to dismantle the faith, they instead were converted to the faith. They would become some of the greatest advocates and defenders of Christianity the world has ever known.

The "Prince of Preachers," Charles Haden Spurgeon, is often quoted as having said, *"The Word of God is like a lion. You don't have to defend a lion. All you have to do is let the lion loose, and the lion will defend itself."* [8]

Enough said, right?

IT IS A DISCERNER, A CRITIC OF HEARTS AND MINDS

My home is filled with a lot of estrogen. I have a wife and two daughters. I bought a couple of male Golden Retrievers just to balance things out a bit. What I'm about to say may be a controversial statement to some of you, but here goes: There is a difference between men and women. We are equal in dignity and value, but God made us wonderfully different. I won't attempt to list out those differences here, but I would like to highlight one you may not have noticed. Men and women approach a mirror differently. When a woman approaches a mirror, you can be assured, something is going to change.

She could be the most beautiful, drop-dead gorgeous woman on the planet and yet, she will find something to fix. Men, on the other hand, approach a mirror and nothing changes. The reflection in the glass could reveal a mess of a man, but when the man looks in the mirror, he thinks "good enough." Whenever we open the Bible, we must approach it like a woman approaches a mirror and not like a man. Something must change. The book of James sums it up well:

> *But be doers of the word, and not hearers only, deceiving yourselves. For if anyone is a hearer of the word and not a doer, he is like a man who looks intently at his natural face in a mirror. For he looks at himself and goes away and at once forgets what he was like. (James 1:22-24 ESV)*

We don't just read the Word, the Word reads us. If we look intently into the mirror, but nothing changes, what's the point? We are not letting the Word do its work. To point out areas of our hearts and minds that God wants to change for our own good and His glory.

IT IS REMARKABLY TRANSLATABLE

I still recall one night while playing for the Hartford Whalers. We had a critical game against a divisional rival. The tension was thick in the locker room. The players rocked back and forth in their seats to release nervous energy, and the room was unusually silent. One of our players, Mikael Anderson, was from Sweden. Along with English being his second language, he was reserved by nature as well. So you can imagine how shocked we all were when he suddenly stood up and blurted out in broken English, "Let's go, guys! It's OK. It's just *'the calm before the weather!'*" After he sat back down, the player seated next to him whispered back, "Bro, I think you mean 'the calm before the storm.'"

Sometimes things get lost in translation, don't they? I heard of one American pastor speaking as a guest at a church in England. As he attempted to win the crowd over with a quick story, he very innocently referenced the fact he was wearing a "fanny pack." The crowd gasped. Apparently in England, the word "fanny" means something entirely different than it does here in the United States and can be quite offensive. Another pastor friend of mine is a pretty animated guy. When he likes something, he'll give you the two thumbs up signal, which is totally appropriate in the United States. But, if you do that in Greece, you're actually giving the person you're communicating with the bird.

See what I mean by getting lost in translation? How incredible is it that the Bible is so timeless and borderless. The themes of sacrifice, love, and rescue resonate deep in the human heart whether you're in Africa or Amsterdam. The Bible is The Story that all other stories point to. Its principles will lead you into abundant life whether you live in India or Indiana.

IT LODGES IN HEARTS AND GROWS. IT TRANSFORMS OTHER LIFE

Ice skating is hard, especially when you're first learning. If you think about it, balancing all your weight on a blade ⅛ inch wide can seem to defy the laws of physics.

Once you do get moving, you can reach speeds of ten to 25 mph. This speed presents the next problem, STOPPING! I remember learning to skate and counting the falls each practice. Slowly but surely, the falls became fewer and fewer, farther and farther apart. Eventually, the falls were transformed into a fourteen-year NHL career.

That's kind of how I'd describe my time with the Bible. One chapter per day, day after day, started to change me from the inside out. I had fewer falls and a stronger faith. The Word of God was slowly changing me from the inside out. It became lodged in my heart, slowly transforming my life.

Charles Spurgeon tells the story of Augustine, an early church father. Augustine was a sex addict prior to his conversion. After becoming a Christian, he famously prayed, "Grant me chastity and temperance…but not yet." [9] These words illustrate a real struggle and honest prayer many young men can identify with. Over time, however, the Word of God and the Holy Spirit began to transform this former sex addict from the inside out. Spurgeon recounts Augustine's dramatic transformation:

> *After his conversion he met with a woman who had been the sharer of his wicked follies; she approached him winningly and said to him, "Augustine," but he ran away from her with all speed. She called after him and said, "Augustine, it is I," mentioning her name; but he then turned round and said, "<u>But it is not I</u>; the old Augustine is dead and I am a new creature in Christ Jesus." [10]*

The Bible is a nonnegotiable for the Christian life. As the Word of God gets in you, it has the power to transform you. It gives you the tools you need to win in life and I want you to win.

Let's leave this section with one last example. It was the '94–'95 NHL season. The New Jersey Devils had a mediocre regular season finishing fifth in the Eastern Conference. The Detroit Red Wings, on the other hand, were a powerhouse, finishing with the best record in the NHL. Something drastically changed during the playoffs though. New Jersey went on an epic run and somehow played like a totally different team. The Devils met the heavily favored Red Wings in the Stanley Cup final. Many were wondering if the series would be a sweep. It was a sweep. . . for the Devils! Nobody saw this shocking upset coming. My friend and former teammate Bobby Holik played for the Devils that season. I asked him about the transformation from an average regular season to Stanley Cup Champion. He gave a simple but profound response: "As players, we stopped trying to do things our own way. We decided to listen to the coach. We followed his game plan and we won. It's that simple."

Here's a great formula for winning a Stanley cup and a great formula for winning in life: Listen to the Coach (God). Follow His game plan (The Bible). And WIN!

CHAPTER 6

"TALKING WITH THE GREAT ONE" (PRAYER)

Now Jesus was praying in a certain place, and when he finished, one of his disciples said to him, "Lord, teach us to pray..."
(Luke 11:1 ESV)

Wayne Douglas Gretzky is the greatest hockey player of all time. No one else really comes close. He holds fifty-seven NHL records, including most goals (894), most assists (1,963) and most total points (2,857). If you were to wipe away all of Gretzky's goals from the record books, he'd still have more total points than any other player. Now you know why they call him, "The Great One."

I remember my first time playing against him. It was October 30, 1991. I was playing for the Hartford Whalers as we hosted Gretzky and the Los Angeles Kings. The game was pretty physical. Bodies were flying all around, and the referees were just trying to keep the players from getting out of control. Too late! An all-out brawl broke out on the ice as all five skaters from each team dropped the gloves and grabbed a member of the opposition. I was matched up with Wayne Gretzky! We grabbed one another as fights broke out around us. I did not want to fight Wayne Gretzky for several reasons:

#1 IT'S WAYNE GRETZKY!

#2 He's not a very big guy at barely 6'0" tall and about 185 pounds. I was 6'2" and 200 pounds. It was a bad look and I wanted no part of it.

I pushed Wayne away and attempted to find another, larger combatant. As I skated away, he once again grabbed hold of my jersey and said, "Let those other guys fight it out. You and I can just watch." Then it hit me! OMG, I'm standing here with Wayne Gretzky. The guy I idolized as a kid. The Great One! We just started talking as chaos ensued all around us. In retrospect, I should have asked him to autograph my stick or something.

Talking with the Great One is the essence of prayer. Simply talking to God. You don't have to speak like Shakespeare using an array of "thee's and thou's." You don't have to pretend to be a theologian or anyone other than yourself. He wants to hear from you. The real you. Prayer is talking to God about what's on your heart and mind.

PRAYER BUILDS RELATIONSHIP WITH GOD

Rejoice always, pray without ceasing, give thanks in all circumstances; for this is the will of God in Christ Jesus for you.
(1 Thessalonians 5:16-18 ESV)

The Apostle Paul challenges us to "pray without ceasing." I don't know about you, but that sounds unreasonable to me, maybe even impossible. I remember early in my Christian faith trying to pray. Five minutes felt like five hours. I ran out of things to talk about very, very quickly. Anyone else?

Hebrews 11 in your Bible is what's known as the "Hall of Fame of Faith." Many of the giants of the Old Testament show up: Abraham, Moses, and David. One character stands out. His name is Enoch.

By faith Enoch was taken up so that he should not see death, and he was not found, because God had taken him. Now before he was taken he was commended as having pleased God.
(Hebrews 11:5 ESV)

Apparently, God liked this guy Enoch so much, He simply took him straight up to heaven. No dying for Enoch. What did he do in order for God to be so fond of him? Let's go back to Genesis and find out.

Enoch <u>walked with God</u>, and he was not, for God took him.
(Genesis 5:24 ESV)

That's it? Enoch "walked with God" seems a bit anticlimactic. "Walking with God" is the Bible's poetic way of saying Enoch lived all of life with God. Everything he did and everywhere he went, Enoch had this awareness of the presence of God with him. Enoch learned to "pray without ceasing" and it pleased the heart of God.

The name Enoch means "disciplined." Discipline characterized his life. He trained himself to walk and talk with God, to pray, and out of the overflow of that discipline, his relationship with God grew. Prayer spilled over into every area of his life.

My wife Susan and I have been happily married for thirty-five years. If I were to talk to her for one hour a week on a Sunday or on Christmas and Easter only, do you think we'd have any shot at staying married? Of course not. No communication, no relationship. It's that simple.

For example, in the UK, the number one reason given for divorce is no longer infidelity. It's "we fell out of love" [1]. I believe that might be the dumbest thing I've ever heard. You don't fall out of love. That would be like me reporting to training camp fat and out of shape, and when confronted by my coach I reply, *"I don't know what happened? I just fell out of shape."* I didn't "fall out of shape." No! I stopped doing the necessary training and disciplines required to stay in great shape. "Falling out of love" works the same way. You must discipline yourself to continually cultivate your relationship with your spouse . . . and with the Lord.

You will never FIND time to pray. You can LOSE time. You can WASTE time. But, you will never FIND time. You can, however, MAKE time. Enoch was a disciplined man who made time to pray. His relationship with God grew and grew. He learned to walk with God, and so can we.

PRAYER: THE ANSWER TO ALL OF LIFE'S PROBLEMS

I don't think I'd ever want to be a head coach in the NHL. There is too much pressure and too much blame. An assistant coach, on the other hand, sounds like a great job to me. For the most part, you can be friendly with the players. Oftentimes, you get to be the "good cop" while the head coach is the "bad cop." I'm convinced assistant coaches don't even need to know much about the game of hockey. One of my old assistant coaches gave one stock answer to every question we presented to him: "It's a read and react situation." Coach, which man should I pick up defensively? "It's a read and react situation." Coach, which man should I cover in front of the net? "It's a read and react situation." Coach, who goes out next shift? "It's a read and react situation." To this day, I can't tell if he simply didn't know the game of hockey or if he was brilliant, because every situation really is a "read and react situation."

After twenty years of pastoring people, I find myself giving the same answer to solve life's problems: PRAY. Maybe it sounds very cliched or even like a cop-out, but it is the right answer. If you don't believe me, take it from the "prophet" Stanley Burrell, also known as "MC Hammer." His smash hit "Pray" beat the drum of prayer over and over again. One hundred and forty-seven times to be exact. "We need to pray just to make it today!"

Another proponent of prayer was James, the Lord's brother. He led the early church in Jerusalem, which was a very difficult job. He needed the power of prayer:

Is anyone among you suffering? Let him pray. Is anyone cheerful? Let him sing praise. Is anyone among you sick? Let him call for the elders of the church, and let them pray over him, anointing him with oil in the name of the Lord. And the prayer of faith will save the one who is sick, and the Lord will raise him up. And if he has committed sins, he will be forgiven. Therefore, confess your sins to one another and pray for one another, that you may be healed. The prayer of a righteous person has great power as it is working. Elijah was a man with a nature like ours, and he prayed fervently that it might not rain, and for three years and six months it did not rain on the earth. Then he prayed again, and heaven gave rain, and the earth bore its fruit. (James 5:13-18 ESV)

James had one answer to all of life's problems: PRAYER. Apparently, he prayed so often his knees grew calloused and knobby like a camel. His nickname became "camel knees" because he prayed with such frequency.

FOUR-SECOND PRAYERS

Kevin Hines struggled with depression for most of his life. Too tired to fight any longer, Kevin decided to end it all. He would jump off the Golden Gate Bridge. For some reason, people tend to romanticize ending their life this way. Roughly thirty people per year make the deadly leap. Your body reaches speeds upwards of 75 mph. When you hit the water, many of your bones shatter and act like shrapnel, puncturing your vital organs. If you survive the impact, you most likely will wind up drowning to death. It takes about four seconds from the moment your feet leave the ground until impact.

Kevin walked to the end of the bridge and jumped. Instant regret hit him as he began to plummet. Kevin recounts, "The thoughts in those four seconds, it was 'What have I just done? I don't want to die. God please save me.'" [2] God hears four-second prayers. Kevin hit the water at 75 mph, shattering several vertebrae. He survived the impact, but now had no use of his legs. Staying afloat was exhausting. Just when he thought it couldn't get any worse, he noticed a dark object lurking in the deep waters beneath him. He thought to himself, I survived the jump, but now I'm going to be eaten by a shark! The shark struck him on the backside. Except, it wasn't a shark at all. It was a sea lion. It was supporting Kevin's lifeless body, keeping him afloat until the Coast Guard arrived. God hears four-second prayers.

The Apostle Peter knows all about four-second prayers. In Matthew 14, the disciples are in a boat crossing the Sea of Galilee at night. A storm rips through and overtakes the unsuspecting sailors. They fear for their lives. That fear would redirect from the storm to a man walking on the water. Jesus tells his exhausted disciples not to be afraid. Peter, still unsure who this "water walker" was, challenges, *"If it's really you, bid me to come walk on the water."* Jesus obliges and Peter walks on water! For a moment, and then he overthinks it. When he sees the wind and the rain, Peter's fear gets the better of him and he starts to sink. Terrified, he throws up a four second prayer:

"...Lord, save me." (Matthew 14:30 ESV)

The Lord reaches out His hand and scoops up the struggling disciple. Jesus answers prayer, even four second prayers. Do you have situations in your life that feel impossible? Pray. It really is the answer to all of life's problems.

PRAYER: LET GOD DO THE HEAVY LIFTING

I had just finished practice and thought I'd get a little extra weight-lifting in. Most of my Philadelphia Flyer teammates had gone home. I had the gym all to myself. I didn't realize how much practice had taken out of me, until I started doing several reps on the bench press. Counting, six, seven, eight, nine, I thought, surely I got one more rep in me. I lowered the 225-pound weight to my chest and tried driving it up for my tenth rep, but my exhausted muscles couldn't lift the weight. I was alone and stuck, buried under a 225-pound barbell. I did the only thing I could think of: yell for HELP! Fortunately, our strength coach was within earshot and gave me a spot. He lifted the heavy burden from off my chest. Are you feeling overwhelmed with life? Like the weight of the world is on your chest? It's time to pray and allow Jesus to do the heavy lifting. The Apostle Peter says:

> . . . *casting all your anxieties on him (Jesus),*
> *because he cares for you. (1 Peter 5:7 ESV)*

Our church is pretty serious when it comes to discipline. We have removed people from ministry before. In the past, we've had to correct some church members around issues like the Trinity, the inerrancy of Scripture, and salvation by grace through faith alone. Along with theological matters, there is one other heresy I will not tolerate in our church. LeBron is NOT the G.O.A.T.! It's MJ! Michael Jordan. End of story. To believe otherwise is to come under severe church discipline. I'm joking, but not really.

March 28, 1990. Michael Jordan and the Chicago Bulls defeated the Cleveland Cavaliers 117–113. Jordan scored an astounding sixty-nine points. Afterwards reporters interviewed Bulls rookie Stacey King, who scored just one point during the contest. When reporters asked what he'd remember most about the game, King replied, "I'll always remember this as the night Michael Jordan and I combined to score seventy points." [3] Jordan did all the heavy lifting for Stacey King and the Bulls. Jesus will do the heavy lifting for you. Roll your care over onto Him in prayer. He cares for you.

GOD ALWAYS ANSWERS PRAYER: YES, NO, NOT YET

And this is the confidence that we have toward him, that if we ask anything according to his will he hears us. And if we know that he hears us in whatever we ask, we know that we have the requests that we have asked of him. (1 John 5:14-15 ESV)

The 2003 film *Bruce Almighty* [4] stars Jim Carrey as TV newsman Bruce Nolan. Bruce thinks God is doing a really crummy job of running the universe and believes he could do better. (I'm glad we've never thought that before.) God, played by Morgan Freeman, decides to give Bruce his shot at being The Almighty. Bruce is loving it. Until, he is inundated with all kinds of prayers filling up his "Inbox." Overwhelmed, he simply responds "YES" to everyone's prayers. Do you remember what happens next? Chaos, pandemonium, and the destruction of life as we know it. God always answers prayer, but not always like we think He should.

We've all prayed prayers that seemingly go unanswered. But it's not true. God always answers prayer. Sometimes we just don't like the answer. The Apostle Paul is a pretty big deal in your Bible. In fact, he wrote a large portion of it! Paul performed miracles and even visited the "third heaven" (2 Corinthians 12:2), Yet, he prayed three times that God would remove a "thorn in the flesh" that had been tormenting him, and God's reply was NO.

Three times I pleaded with the Lord about this, that it should leave me. But he said to me, "My grace is sufficient for you, for my power is made perfect in weakness." (2 Corinthians 12:8-9 ESV)

Jesus, in the Garden of Gethsemane, prays three times to His heavenly Father that the cup of suffering might pass from Him. The answer was NO. I'm guessing if God told Paul and Jesus NO, there is a pretty good chance He will say NO to some of our prayers too.

Sometimes the answer isn't NO, it's simply NOT YET. In other words, God's timing and our timing aren't the same. According to pastor and author Mark Batterson, there are a total number of 169,518,829,100,544,000,000,000,000,000 possible permutations in just the first ten moves of a chess game. [5] If that is the case for a simple chess game, how many possible moves are on the board for God on any given day? He's got a lot going on in the universe. Every decision impacts all the other pieces on the board.

I believe Pastor Tim Keller sums up God's "NOT YET" best: "God will only give you what you would have asked for if you knew everything He knows." [6] Maybe your NO is actually only a NOT YET.

Sometimes the answer to prayer is YES! God is a good God and loves to give good gifts to His kids. Jesus says:

"If you then, who are evil, know how to give good gifts to your children, how much more will your Father who is in heaven give good things to those who ask him!" (Matthew 7:11 ESV)

Grab hold of "The Great One" in prayer and don't let go. Your YES is on its way. Prayer is how we win in the Christian life, and I want you to win.

CHAPTER 7

"POWER" (THE HOLY SPIRIT)

"But you will receive power when the Holy Spirit has come upon you, and you will be my witnesses in Jerusalem and in all Judea and Samaria, and to the end of the earth." (Acts 1:8 ESV)

I was really never much of a video game guy. But when *NHL 95* was released and I found out I was in the game, I quickly became a gamer. The thrill of being in an actual video game quickly faded to frustration. My avatar was terrible. Absolute trash. I wasn't fast. I wasn't tough or skilled. I found out later that there is actually a "power ranking" for each player in the game. Each player gets a number from one to one hundred, one being the lowest and one hundred being the highest. I was a fifty-six!! C'mon man! Is that even a passing grade? Surely I was better than a "fifty-six"? Nope.

I soon discovered that my friends, who were seasoned gamers, could win with my avatar despite my dreadfully low ranking. Sure, I was a fifty-six, but with them in control I was so much more. I was good. Really good. And that's a picture of how the Christian life is supposed to work. All of us, if we were honest, are just a bunch of fifty-sixers. But if we will give control of our life over to the Holy Spirit, we can be so much more!

The God of Christianity reveals Himself as a "Trinity," a "Tri-Unity." Think of this as Three Whos: Father, Son, and Spirit, and One What: God. For the most part, humanity understands the concept of God the Father and God the Son. God the Holy Spirit, however, can be confusing and at times even divisive amongst Christians. If I were the Devil, I would want you to remain confused and reluctant about the Spirit, too. The Holy Spirit empowers us to live the Christian life. He takes our fifty-six and turns it into something powerful, something supernatural.

Early in my Christian walk, a friend shared with me three simple words that helped me understand the role of the Holy Spirit in my life. Those three words are: "With", "In," and "Upon."

THE HOLY SPIRIT **WITH** YOU BEFORE SALVATION

"Nevertheless, I tell you the truth: it is to your advantage that I go away, for if I do not go away, the Helper will not come to you. But if I go, I will send him to you. And when he comes, he will convict the world concerning sin and righteousness and judgment."
(John 16:7-8 ESV)

Jesus actually said that it is to our advantage that He goes away so He can send "the Helper," the Holy Spirit. The word "Helper" in the original Greek language is "paraklētos." which literally means one "called alongside." The Spirit comes alongside you and helps.

After falling down two games to none in the 2002–2003 NBA playoffs, the Portland Trail Blazers headed back home for game three. Trail Blazers fans packed the stadium in hopes of cheering their team to its first victory in the series against the Dallas Mavericks. Thirteen-year-old Natalie Gilbert was scheduled to sing the national anthem. Young Natalie grabbed the mic as the anxious crowd awaited. She awkwardly and nervously begins to sing. The more aware she becomes of the crowd, the less aware she becomes of the lyrics. Finally, she just blanks. She stops singing. The packed arena was eerily silent as the terrified little girl stood all alone in front of some 20,000 fans.

She was all alone, until one man came up beside her. It was Portland coach and former player Maurice "Mo" Cheeks. He put an arm around her and picked up the lyrics where she had left off. As he sang, his eyes invited young Natalie to join in.

The solo had become a duet. The crowd was so moved, they too joined in until the entire stadium sang in unison, ". . . and the home of the braaaaave!" The game hadn't even started yet, but everyone already felt like they'd won. [1] One man stepped forward, stood beside Natalie, and turned disaster into triumph. The Helper is the one called alongside to support and guide us in our time of need. That is the role of the Holy Spirit.

The Helper helps us to see and know Jesus. Do you have good vision? Late in my NHL career, I could feel my eyesight beginning to deteriorate. LASIK surgery was relatively new at the time, but I thought it could help my vision, so I decided to give it a try. I've had several surgeries over the years, but nothing compared to this one. It didn't hurt at all. It was what I call a "toe curler." It's just kinda gross and freaks you out a bit. The procedure is quick, but it will make you squirm. The surgical nurses lay you on a table and put a device on your eyelids to keep them open. LASIK surgery uses a laser to burn and reshape the cornea. When that laser hits your eye, you can literally smell smoke! As they are peeling back part of the cornea you are momentarily blinded. It will make your toes curl. Before panic sets in, the reshaped cornea is put back into place and you can see again!

Spiritual blindness plagues all of us. We need the help of the Holy Spirit to see. For example, both Luke 22 and John 18 describe the arrest of Jesus. The arresting soldiers ask for Jesus by name, to which He replies, "I am He." With those words, power flows out of the Son of God and all the soldiers are knocked to the ground. They get up, dust themselves off and move forward with the arrest. Really? Wouldn't that kind of incident make you pause for a moment and wonder, "Maybe this Jesus guy is legit"?

It gets better. As one of the soldiers moves in to arrest Jesus, Peter, full of himself, pulls a sword and chops off the guy's ear. Jesus picks up the dismembered ear and puts it back on the guy's head! What happens next is bewildering; the soldiers move forward with the arrest! Do you see what I mean by being blind? A miracle just happened before their very eyes, and they didn't truly see it.

In John 11, Jesus raises a man named Lazarus from the dead. He was four days in the grave before Jesus arrived on the scene. Jesus stood before the tomb and called out, "Lazarus come forth!" Lazarus emerges from the grave alive! Can we agree that if someone says they are the Son of God and raises a man from the dead, you might at least have to consider that it might be true? Not the Pharisees (the religious elite that hated Jesus). Instead, they decided not only to kill Jesus, but that they needed to kill Lazarus as well! They were blind to ultimate reality right in front of them. But to those who are willing to believe, the Holy Spirit gives spiritual sight.

Every Christmas we remember the three wise men from the East. For the record, the Bible never tells us how many wise men there were. Most assume three because of the three gifts they brought to baby Jesus: gold, frankincense, and myrrh. Jesus was most likely not even a baby when they arrived. He was probably about two years old. As they followed the star, the wise men arrived at Jesus' home and here was their response:

And going into the house they saw the child with Mary his mother, and they fell down and worshiped him. Then, opening their treasures, they offered him gifts, gold and frankincense and myrrh. (Matthew 2:11 ESV)

I don't know about you, but I've met a lot of two-year-olds. I've never once felt compelled to worship any of them. What was different? These men were given eyes to see the one *"born King of the Jews."* (Matthew 2:2)

In Luke 23, Jesus has been brutally beaten and hung on a cross between two thieves. Jesus is barely recognizable as a man, let alone as the Son of God. Yet, one of the thieves is given eyes to see beyond the crown of thorns and bloodied face. He sees Jesus as the King of Kings:

And he said, "Jesus, remember me when you come into your kingdom." And He said to him, "Truly, I say to you, today you will be with me in Paradise." (Luke 23:42-43 ESV)

The Helper is *with* you before your salvation, giving you spiritual eyes to see Jesus as He is. The Spirit is also *with* us to convict of "sin, righteousness and judgement" (John 16:8).

Back in 2006, the Indianapolis Colts were in town to take on the New York Giants. I was asked to lead the chapel service for the Colts. Hall of Fame Coach Tony Dungy was in attendance. If you're not familiar with his story, Coach Dungy has a son with a rare neurological condition that prohibits him from feeling pain. At first glance, this sounds awesome. No pain sounds incredible. It isn't. In fact, it's horrible. Without pain acting as a warning signal for danger, his son is constantly harming himself.

Coach Dungy describes one instance when his wife was baking cookies. His son, only five years old at the time, smelled the delightful treats baking in the 350 degree oven. When his mom wasn't looking, he opened the oven door and grabbed the hot cookie sheet, burning his young hands, and then placed the bubbling hot cookie dough into his mouth. The fiery dough scalded his tongue and mouth badly. But he felt nothing. Because he doesn't feel pain, he hurts himself again and again. [2]

This story, as sad as it is, might help us understand how the Holy Spirit comes to keep us from harming ourselves and others through sin. We can define "sin" as bad things we do that we know we shouldn't do. The Holy Spirit, through love, sometimes produces pain in order to make us see, to bring us back to righteousness. The Apostle Paul calls this spiritual pain "godly grief."

For godly grief produces a repentance that leads to salvation without regret, whereas worldly grief produces death.
(2 Corinthians 7:10 ESV)

When the Holy Spirit is with you, it's virtually impossible to enjoy your sin. The feeling of godly grief warns us to avoid it. To ignore the conviction of the Holy Spirit is to harm yourself and to grieve the Holy Spirit. If you ignore the Spirit enough, you develop what the Bible calls a "hardened heart." You lose the ability to feel the Holy Spirit with you.

THE HOLY SPIRIT IN YOU AT SALVATION

In him you also, when you heard the word of truth, the gospel of your salvation, and believed in him, were sealed with the promised Holy Spirit, who is the guarantee of our inheritance until we acquire possession of it, to the praise of his glory.
(Ephesians 1:13-14 ESV)

NHL players are so spoiled today. Their equipment is so far superior to the stuff we used back in the day. But I guess you can say that about almost anything these days. Remember when the telephone used to be something attached to the wall? Now, we take them everywhere with us. Back in the day, you actually had to memorize people's phone numbers or look them up in something called a "phone book." Remember those? To take a photograph, you needed an actual camera that used actual film. After you snapped the picture, you had to wait until the film was fully used. Then you had to take it to a Kodak store or pharmacy to have the film developed. After waiting for a week or two, the photos would finally be ready. You'd have to drive back to the pharmacy and pick up the photos, only to find out your finger was over part of the lens for the majority of the shots. Today, however, our cameras are on our phones. We get to see the photos immediately. That's progress!

Progress isn't a new phenomenon. In the Old Testament, in order to meet with God, all kinds of animals had to be sacrificed and various ceremonial washings took place to create "clean spaces" where God and man could meet. Moses had the Tent of Meeting where only he and Aaron, the priest could enter. Later, Solomon would build the Temple. In the center of the Temple was the Holy of Holies. Here dwelt the tangible presence of God. A giant veil four inches thick separated sinful man from the Most Holy Place. Once a year, after a series of sacrifices and washings, only one man, the high priest, could enter the Holy of Holies.

Fast-forward to Jesus and the New Testament. Jesus arrives on the scene, lives perfectly as our "High Priest" and dies on the cross in our place as our sacrifice. When he does, Matthew records what happens to the Temple veil:

> *And behold, the curtain of the temple was torn in two, from top to bottom. (Matthew 27:51 ESV)*

The Spirit of God was made directly, personally, available to us. After His resurrection, Jesus breathed on his disciples and said, "Receive the Holy Spirit." The presence of God no longer dwells in tents or temples. YOU have become "clean space." YOU are the temple of God through the work of Jesus on the cross. If you don't believe me, believe the Apostle Paul:

Or do you not know that your body is a temple of the Holy Spirit within you, whom you have from God? You are not your own.
(1 Corinthians 6:19 ESV)

Now that's progress. The Old Testament heroes would be so envious of all we have received through the cross of Jesus Christ. Men like Moses and David would be floored. I can hear them now, "The Holy Spirit dwells where? In human hearts?"

When you receive Jesus Christ, you are immediately "sealed" with the Holy Spirit. He is in you. Nothing and no one can separate you from God's Holy Spirit. Your relationship to God is changed fully and forever.

CHILDREN OF GOD

I'm the proud father of two daughters. Each time one of my girls was born, I remember thinking two things:

1) I never knew I could love something as deeply and unconditionally as I do my kids.

2) Thank GOD I'm a MAN!

Mom's are so amazing. If dudes had to have babies, forget about it. Just think about all moms endure on behalf of their unborn children: morning sickness, sleepless nights, food aversions, and weight gain. My wife and I were looking at some old photos from her first pregnancy. She retained so much water that I told her it looked like she was carrying the baby in her face! (Men, please learn from my mistakes.)

Then, comes the pain of childbirth. Giving birth involves literally hours of horrific pain and pushing, until finally, the child is born. Here is the sad reality for almost every mom. After all they go through to bring this child into the world, the first words out of your kid's mouth will be "Dada." Sorry, moms, but it's true.

The same is true for you when you are "born again." When you become a Christian, the Holy Spirit testifies to your spirit that you are a child of God. The first sound, the first utterance of your spirit is to call God your Father:

But you have received the Spirit of adoption as sons, by whom we cry, "Abba! Father!" The Spirit himself bears witness with our spirit that we are children of God. (Romans 8:15-16 ESV)

RESTORATION AND RENOVATION

My cable TV provider supplies me with access to over 200 channels. The reality is we only use three: ESPN, Food Network, and HGTV. If you pay attention, HGTV is basically the same show over and over again. See if this sounds familiar: An old home, we'll call it a "fixer upper," needs work to be restored. The cost for restoration is estimated and then demolition begins. Midway into the demo, "Oh no! We have a problem!" Cut to commercial. Back to the program, there is always some unforeseen problem that will add five grand to the budget. Problem is fixed, and the renovation continues. After a lot of blood, sweat, and tears, we get the big reveal. "OMG!! It's BEAUTIFUL!!" Tears begin to flow, and the credits roll.

We are all "Fixer Uppers," and the Holy Spirit *in* you, immediately begins to renovate you from the inside out. The Prophet Ezekiel says it this way:

"And I will give you a new heart, and a new spirit I will put within you. And I will remove the heart of stone from your flesh and give you a heart of flesh. And I will put my Spirit within you, and cause you to walk in my statutes and be careful to obey my rules." (Ezekiel 36:26-27 ESV)

The Holy Spirit will give you a new heart, a heart that loves what Jesus loves and hates what Jesus hates. If I'm honest, there are still some things my heart is drawn to that God calls wicked. I must wrestle against those desires, but not forever. I know the Holy Spirit is inside me changing those desires and appetites to align with His. Unlike an HGTV show, the renovation is never over. The Holy Spirit's work goes on.

THE HOLY SPIRIT **UPON** YOU WITH POWER

"But you will receive power when the Holy Spirit has come upon you, and you will be my witnesses in Jerusalem and in all Judea and Samaria, and to the end of the earth." (Acts 1:8 ESV)

You'd be surprised how many people in professional sports have "Dad Bods." Guys you look at and wonder: 'How on earth are they actually professional athletes?' I played with one of those guys. The moment you saw this guy with his shirt off you thought, "That guy has more rolls than a bakery!" But, after one off season, he came back absolutely ripped. He was lean and muscular. I had to ask him what he was doing to get such great results? He told me he quit eating bread! Like an idiot, I believed him and cut out all bread from my diet. Nothing! No change. Come to find out a few years later, that same guy got busted for using P.E.D.'s (Performance Enhancing Drugs). No bread, right?

The Holy Spirit is God's P.E.D for His people. He promised to send the Holy Spirit and power to be His witness. The Holy Spirit is "*With* You" before salvation. He is "*In* You" at salvation. And will come "*Upon* You" for the necessary power to be His witness.

At the beginning of this chapter, I highlighted the fact I'm a fifty-six. But with the Holy Spirit *upon* me, I'm so much more. In fact all the heroes you read about in the Bible are just a bunch of fifty-sixes. Yet with the Holy Spirit *upon* them, they become so much more.

For example, Moses was just a guy shepherding sheep. He stuttered and had anger issues: In a rage he killed an Egyptian with his bare hands. Furious at his own people, Moses shattered the stone tablets with the Ten Commandments written on them. Angered again at his people, he struck the Rock when God told him to speak to it. You see, Moses really was just a fifty-six like you and me. But with the Holy Spirit upon him, God used him to deliver a nation.

Here's another example. David had "daddy issues." When David's father, Jesse, was asked to bring all his sons before the Prophet Samuel, he brought all seven of his sons except for David, whom he left out in the field. Thanks dad!

In his writings David comes across as being schizophrenic. We all know Psalm 23 *"The Lord is my shepherd I shall not want...."* David also wrote the one right before it, Psalm 22. It begins, *"My God, my God, why have you forsaken me?"* See what I mean by schizophrenic? David was a "fifty-six" like you and me. But, with the Holy Spirit upon him, David was a powerhouse. He killed lions and bears with his bare hands. He slew giants and established the Kingdom. God even called him "a man after My own heart."

All twelve of the disciples would be ranked at fifty-six—maybe less. Peter may have been more like a forty-eight. On the night Jesus is arrested and tried, Peter follows the events from a distance. As he warms himself beside a fire, a young girl accuses him of being a follower of Jesus, which he vehemently denies. Others press him, saying, "You were with him." He again denies, swearing, "I do not know Him!" At that very moment, Jesus, in chains, looks across the courtyard and locks eyes with Peter. At this point, he's well below a fifty-six.

After the day of Pentecost, however, the Holy Spirit would come upon Peter. This same man who, weeks earlier, was such a coward, boldly proclaims the Gospel and 3,000 people are added to the church. The same man that denied he even knew Jesus, points his finger in the face of those that crucified Jesus and declares:

> *"Let all the house of Israel therefore know for certain that God has made him both Lord and Christ, this Jesus whom you crucified."*
> *(Acts 2:36 ESV)*

You see? God can take a bunch of fifty-sixes and put His Spirit UPON them and absolutely change the world.

I'll end this chapter with the story of a young youth pastor named Richard. At age twenty-five, Richard hit a really dark season of life. He fell into a deep depression so severe he had to be hospitalized. His therapist asked him the question, "What are you so mad about?" as depression can often be the result of unresolved anger. He had no answer.

Upon being released from the hospital, a kind church member offered Richard a small, remote cabin in the woods as a retreat. Richard's time alone only seemed to make things worse. One frightful evening, Richard awoke from a horrible nightmare. In it, demons were tormenting him. At his wit's end, Richard said out loud, "I think I'm losing my mind." Not long after that declaration, the phone rang. Richard was startled. Nobody knew where he was staying. He hadn't given the phone number to anyone. Puzzled, he slowly lifted the receiver and said, "Hello?" The voice on the other end was unfamiliar and very direct, "You don't know me, but God told me to call you. He wanted me to remind you of 2 Timothy 1:7." Then he quoted the Scripture:

For God hath not given us the spirit of fear; but of power, and of love, and of a sound mind. (2 Timothy 1:7 KJV)

The man hung up the phone, and Richard has never been the same. Those words not only healed his anxious soul, they reminded him of the Spirit that rests upon him. The Spirit of power, love and a *sound mind* <u>restored him</u>. Richard would go on to do some amazing things with his life. You might know him better as Pastor Rick Warren. He's the bestselling author of *The Purpose Driven Life*. He also founded Saddleback Church which has an average weekly attendance of 30,000 people. He has advised presidents and has been referred to as "America's Pastor." [3] If the Holy Spirit can do that for young Richard, what might he do for you?

Do you want the Power of God upon your life? All you have to do is ask your heavenly Father:

"What father among you, if his son asks for a fish, will instead of a fish give him a serpent; or if he asks for an egg, will give him a scorpion? If you then, who are evil, know how to give good gifts to your children, how much more will the heavenly Father give the Holy Spirit to those who ask him!" (Luke 11:11-13 ESV)

The Holy Spirit can take your fifty-six and do more than you could ever think, dream, or imagine. He will give you the power necessary to win in the Christian life. I want you to win.

CHAPTER 8

"TEAMMATES" (THE CHURCH)

"On this rock I will build my church, and the gates of hell shall not prevail against it." (Matthew 16:18 ESV)

Often athletic teams will have a team song for the season, an anthem. Take the 2019 St. Louis Blues for example. They won their franchise's first ever Stanley Cup Championship riding on the wings of a song that may surprise you. Midway through the season the team was mired in mediocrity. They fired their head coach and still couldn't get on track. All that would change one fateful evening prior to their game against Philadelphia. A group of Blue's players went to a local bar in Philly to watch some football and maybe indulge in a few chicken wings. Each time someone scored a touchdown on the TVs, the bar would crank up the song "Gloria" by Laura Branigan. It got stuck in the players, heads and they couldn't shake it. The following evening St. Louis shutout the Philadelphia Flyers 3–0. After the victory, they blasted "Gloria" on the team's sound system and it instantly became their anthem. They went on an epic winning streak going from worst to first.

"Gloria"-mania captured the hearts of the people of St. Louis and they rode the momentum all the way to the Stanley Cup finals where they defeated the Boston Bruins in seven games. *"Gloria! Gloria!"* [1]

The 1979 Pittsburgh Pirates of Major League Baseball had a similar story. The Pirates were a lackluster team going nowhere. One rain-delayed evening, Pirates Team Captain Willie Stargell was lounging in the dugout killing time when a song came on over the stadium's loudspeaker that caught his attention. The song was "We Are Family" by Sister Sledge. Stargell picked up the dugout phone and immediately called the team's PR Director, informing him this would be the team's new anthem. The song united the players and the city. Pittsburgh went on to shock the baseball world by winning the World Series, defeating the heavily favored Baltimore Orioles four games to three. [2] The celebration rolled out from the Pirate's locker room into the streets of the Steel City. "We Are Family" could be heard from every street corner. It was their song and it's ours as well. When you become a Christian, God makes you part of His family. We Are Family:

> ***See what kind of love the Father has given to us,***
> ***that we should be called children of God. (1 John 3:1 ESV)***

The human heart longs for family. It's hardwired into us as image bearers of God. In fact, God Himself is a family: Father, Son, and Spirit. Think of that, at the center of the universe is a family, and through the cross of Christ we are adopted into that family. We not only get God as our Father, we get a new spiritual family.

TEAMMATES: "SPIRITUAL FAMILY"

Trades are an odd part of pro sports. What other occupation swaps employees? Imagine going to your job at Microsoft and you find out you've been traded to Apple. Or you are working part time at Starbucks and discover they traded you to Dunkin' Donuts. That would be weird, right? A former teammate of mine was once traded for a bus! Not even for another human being. He was instantly nicknamed "Bus-ee." See what I mean, it can get very strange.

I remember the day I was traded from the Carolina Hurricanes to the Philadelphia Flyers. I was in Florida with the Canes to take on the Panthers. The morning of the game I received a call from our head coach, Paul Maurice. He thanked me for my services and informed me I'd been traded to Philadelphia. That day Philly was in Buffalo to play the Sabres, so I jumped on a plane and flew to Buffalo to meet my new teammates.

Here is what's so odd about being traded: Several of my new teammates and I had fought before! Keith Jones and I fought in Washington (I want a rematch with him), and Rick Tocchet and I fought several times. Rick was the one that shattered my cheek. (I DON'T want a rematch with him!) Rod Brind'Amour and I had literally fought one another the week prior to my being traded! These guys who were formerly my enemies had suddenly become my brothers. I used to fight with them, now I would fight for them. We were teammates.

As a Christian, you were traded from the Kingdom of Darkness to the Kingdom of Light. You were traded from Death to Life. You play for a new team. You get new teammates:

> *For as many of you as were baptized into Christ have put on Christ. There is neither Jew nor Greek, there is neither slave nor free, there is no male and female, for you are all one in Christ Jesus. (Galatians 3:27-28 ESV)*

You *"put on Christ"* like a jersey. You become part of His team. Notice how different each of these people are: different ethnicities (Jew and Greek), different social classes (slave and free), different biologies (male and female). And yet, in Christ they are one. Despite all these differences they are ONE team, Team Jesus. We no longer fight with one another. We fight *for* one another. We no longer *divide* over our differences. Instead, we *celebrate* them. We are family. We are the Church.

ADVICE FROM THE TEACHER

Harvard recently released the findings of an eighty-five-year study. The researchers hoped to unlock the secret to happiness and long life. After years of study, they boiled it down to one thing, *life giving relationships*. I could have saved them millions of dollars and years of research by having them read Ecclesiastes. The book of Ecclesiastes is located in the middle of the Old Testament. "Ecclesiastes" simply means, "Preacher" or "Teacher." "The Teacher" gives us the secret to winning in life, Spiritual Teammates.

Two are better than one, because they have a good reward for their toil. For if they fall, one will lift up his fellow. But woe to him who is alone when he falls and has not another to lift him up! Again, if two lie together, they keep warm, but how can one keep warm alone? And though a man might prevail against one who is alone, two will withstand him-a threefold cord is not quickly broken.
(Ecclesiastes 4:9-12 ESV)

As the Teacher of this passage makes clear, belonging to a team, a local church, will increase your PRODUCTION, PROTECTION, PASSION, and POWER.

THE CHURCH WILL INCREASE YOUR *PRODUCTION*

Two are better than one, because they have a good reward for their toil. (Ecclesiastes 4:9)

Prior to being drafted to the NHL, I played for the North Bay Centennials of the Ontario Hockey League (OHL). We had a less than stellar regular season and barely made the final playoff spot for our division. We were slated to play against the best team in all of Canada, the Kitchener Rangers. Our coach called a team meeting to strategize how we could beat this juggernaut. Coach quietly scanned the room and finally asked, "How can we defeat the Rangers?" No one dared suggest we could just out-skill them. They were far superior. One player broke the silence and answered, "We will out-tough them, Coach!" To which Coach responded, "Nope, they are tougher than you." Another teammate quickly jumped in, "Out-skate them Coach! Use our speed." This answer, too, was immediately shot down by Coach. I remember thinking, "Hey, 'Debbie downer', if you're trying to make this playoff feel hopeless, you're doing a bang-up job!"

After shooting down all of our suggestions, he finally presented a solution: "The only possible way you can beat this team is on the POWER PLAY." For those unfamiliar with that term, it's when the other team takes a penalty and plays shorthanded. You get an extra attacker!

Our entire team bought into the game plan. The series began. We stayed disciplined. They took penalties. And our power play took over! We scorched our opponent with the extra attacker. Not only did we beat the Rangers, we humiliated them winning the series four games to one. It's the power of playing with extra attackers. It improves your PRODUCTION. God's spiritual team, the Church, has always been God's plan to change the world. By joining a local church, you increase the impact you can have on the world around you.

Columnist and open atheist Matthew Parris wrote an eye-opening column entitled, *"As an Atheist, I Truly Believe Africa Needs God."* [3] Parris highlights that, unlike traditional NGOs and other nonprofits, the Christian Church not only fixes problems, it transforms people.

"Now a confirmed atheist, I've become convinced of the enormous contribution that Christian evangelism makes in Africa: sharply distinct from the work of secular NGOs, government projects and international aid efforts. These alone will not do. Education and training alone will

not do. <u>In Africa Christianity changes people's hearts.</u> It brings a spiritual transformation. The rebirth is real. The change is good."

Systemic change is taking place in Africa. As churches are planted, people are changed. Transformed hearts lead to transformed homes, cities, and schools. The change is real and lasting. So much so, that an atheist must admit, the Church increases your PRODUCTION.

The Church is at work in Africa, and it's also at work in Possum Trot, Texas. (Yes, that's really a place.) A small rural church in East Texas, pastored by Reverend W. C. Martin and his wife, Donna, single-handedly did away with the need for foster care in the region. Donna Martin received a calling from God to foster and adopt a few children. As she and her husband obeyed God, the vision for fostering children grew in their tiny church. Eventually, all seventy-six of the children that were in the local foster care system were fostered and adopted by members of the small church. [4] This is a story of productivity at its best. One church obeyed God and together, as a team, the church family did away with the need for foster care in East Texas. This powerful story captured the attention of writer/director Joshua Weigel who converted it to the Big Screen. *Sound of Hope: The Story of Possum Trot* is a film that illustrates the power of the local church. [5] It will increase your PRODUCTION.

THE CHURCH WILL INCREASE YOUR PROTECTION

For if they fall, one will lift up his fellow. But woe to him who is alone when he falls and has not another to lift him up!
(Ecclesiastes 4:10 ESV)

It's known as "the Battle at Kruger." On YouTube you can watch this fascinating amateur video shot at Kruger National Park in South Africa. [6] It begins with a massive herd of Cape buffalo roaming the prairie. A young calf wanders away from the herd. (Can you sense where this is headed?)

Off in the tall grass sits a pride of lions. They spot the lone calf and the hunt begins! Sensing danger, the small calf tries to get back to the herd, but it's too late. A pair of lions chase the youngster to the shore of a small pond, and they take the animal to the ground. Just when you think it couldn't get any worse for this calf, a crocodile lunges out of the pond and grabs it! We now are witnessing a lion and a crocodile playing tug of war with this poor baby calf. (If you ever feel like you're having a bad day, remember this poor guy. You'll feel better about your day.)

Just as all seems to be lost for the young buffalo, the scene suddenly shifts. The crocodile abruptly drops its victim and swims away. The lions sense something is approaching behind them. They too let go of the young calf. Turning around, they find a massive herd of buffalo inching towards them. The lions are outweighed, outnumbered, and about to be undone. A massive bull from the herd charges one of the lions, and with one powerful blow sends the cat soaring into the sky. The other feline wants no part of this unwinnable contest and runs away.

When the dust settles, unbelievably, the young calf stands and meanders back into the safety and security of the herd. And that is a picture of spiritual family! When your life feels like it's coming undone, when attacks seem to be coming at you from every direction, God gives us the Church. Spiritual teammates to step in and fight on our behalf. Belonging to the Church will increase your PROTECTION.

The Apostle Peter warns us:

Be sober-minded; be watchful. Your adversary the devil prowls around like a roaring lion, seeking someone to devour.
(1 Peter 5:8 ESV)

Like a roaring lion, the Devil will try to isolate you and then annihilate you. Do you have spiritual teammates that will be there for you in your time of need? King David was a mighty warrior, but he was no Lone Ranger. He may have killed lions and bears and slayed a giant, but David, like all of us, had moments when he was tired and weary. One such moment can be found in 2 Samuel 21:

There was war again between the Philistines and Israel, and David went down together with his servants, and they fought against the Philistines. And David grew weary. And Ishbi-benob, one of the descendants of the giants, whose spear weighed three hundred shekels of bronze, and who was armed with a new sword, thought to kill David. But Abishai the son of Zeruiah came to his aid and attacked the Philistine and killed him.
(2 Samuel 21:15-17 ESV)

In David's time of weakness, he had others around him to fight with him and on his behalf. Abishai fought for David when David could no longer fight for himself. The name "Abishai" means *"gift from the Father."* When we belong to a local church, we surround ourselves with spiritual teammates, "Gifts from the Father." Why would you rob yourself of that and try to walk alone?

In another instance, David finds himself on the run from King Saul, hunted like an animal. Growing weary, hopelessness starts to settle in. Have you been there before? I know I have. But David had a teammate and friend named Jonathan:

And Jonathan, Saul's son, rose and went to David at Horesh, and strengthened his hand in God. And he said to him, "Do not fear, for the hand of Saul my father shall not find you. You shall be king over Israel, and I shall be next to you. (1 Samuel 23:16-17 ESV)

David was on the verge of quitting, giving up. But Jonathan was there to "strengthen his hand in God." Do you have others in your life to strengthen your hand in God? David became the greatest King Israel has ever known, thanks in part to his friend and teammate Jonathan. Do you have a Jonathan in your life? Do you belong to a Church? Finding your spiritual family, your teammates in Christ, will increase your PROTECTION.

THE CHURCH WILL INCREASE YOUR PASSION

Again, if two lie together, they keep warm, but how can one keep warm alone? (Ecclesiastes 4:11 ESV)

It was the 2011 NFL season, my fourth year as New York Jets chaplain. We were in the thick of a playoff run and scheduled to play our cross town rivals, the New York Giants. Coach Rex Ryan asked if I'd lead the team in the Lord's Prayer prior to taking the field. The players, coaches, and I grasped hands and reverently dropped to one knee. The room was silent as the players looked to me to begin the prayer. Then it hit me....I hope I remember the Lord's Prayer! I started, *"Our Father who art in heaven...."* The men joined in baritone unison reciting the prayer until we all arrived at *"Amen!"*

As the men all rose to their feet, Rex gave me the nod to exit the room. The instant the door slammed behind me, the locker room erupted with a mixture of "F-bombs" and various ways they were going to kick the Giants . . . *butt*. That's not the word they used, but this is a Christian book, and I'm a pastor. If you were wondering, we lost the game.

Another type of prayer takes place prior to Most NFL games. It's called the "Shower-Up" prayer. Minutes before the coach's final pump-up speech, the players that love Jesus gather in the locker room shower in full equipment as they prepare to take the field. A designated player prays a short boisterous prayer followed by a collective "amen."

I was invited to join one of the "shower-up" prayers. As the prayer leader passionately declared the Word of God over us in the name of Jesus, I could feel the hair on the back of my neck standing up. A feeling of might started to bubble up on the inside of me. By the time we said "amen" and left that shower, I was ready to hit someone! The enthusiasm of the team members was overwhelming. In fact, the word "enthusiasm" comes from the root word "en-theos" which means "in God." As we gather together in God, an enthusiasm for life is produced in our hearts. PASSION is stirred when we gather together as spiritual teammates, the church family. It's contagious.

And let us consider how to stir up one another to love and good works, not neglecting to meet together, as is the habit of some, but encouraging one another, and all the more as you see the Day drawing near. (Hebrews 10:24-25 ESV)

Something spiritual and powerful happens when believers gather. We are stirred to love and good works. In other words, I'm inspired to be a better man, a better husband, a better father and friend. We each encourage one another.

Think about that, the church is a place where courage is given and received, and all you have to do is show up! Courage to fight the good fight of faith. Courage to do the right thing. Courage to love God and people. I need other faith-filled people in my life to stir my courage and PASSION for God. You see, fear is free, but faith takes work. Both faith and fear are highly contagious and can be caught simply by proximity. God was so serious about quarantining fear that He prohibited cowardly, fearful soldiers from entering battle:

And the officers shall speak further to the people, and say, "Is there any man who is fearful and fainthearted? Let him go back to his house, lest he make the heart of his fellows melt like his own." (Deuteronomy 20:8 ESV)

Fear is the default setting of the world. It's everywhere. Faith, on the other hand, must be cultivated. You must be strategic in surrounding your life with people of faith. Both faith and fear are contagious, which one will you catch?

Jesus chose twelve men of faith to accompany him and share his life's work. His passion and faith infected them. Those twelve disciples infected 120 in an upper room praying after the resurrection. Peter on the day of Pentecost infected 3,000 people with a passion and faith for Jesus. Today, there are roughly 2.38 billion people infected with faith and passion for Jesus. PASSION is contagious. Who are you surrounding yourself with? Who will share your passion?

RUN WITH SPIRITUAL THOROUGHBREDS

What's your favorite movie? It's a question I like to ask. If you're a dude, you need to know the "Trinity" of guy movies: *300*, *Gladiator*, and *Braveheart*. If you think otherwise, you're wrong! But there's another one you should watch. When I asked a friend what his favorite movie was, he said, *"Seabiscuit." Seabiscuit,* seriously? What a lame choice, I thought to myself. And then I watched the movie. It is really good.

The film tells the true story of Seabiscuit, an undersized, unimpressive thoroughbred that finds a bond with his jockey, Red. Together they start winning races and winning in life. This underdog thoroughbred captures the hearts and imagination of the world. The movie crescendos with a showdown between Seabiscuit and the Triple Crown winner War Admiral. Red is injured and unable to race Seabiscuit. He must train another jockey to ride this magical horse. Red coaches his new pupil, telling him to let Seabiscuit get out fast, but to beware, War Admiral likes to close strong at the end.

The game plan takes an odd turn as Red advises to pull back on Seabiscuit down the stretch. 'Let him make eye contact with War

Admiral. When he sees another horse running next to him, he finds a different gear. He goes to another level.'

The race plays out exactly as planned. As the two horses come down the stretch, War Admiral is running stride for stride with Seabiscuit. That is, until Seabiscuit sees his opponent running next to him. BAM! Seabiscuit hits another gear and pulls away, winning the race by four lengths. [7]

I don't know about you, but I want to run with spiritual thoroughbreds. I want to surround myself with men and women of faith that push me to go further and faster in my walk with God, men and women who challenge me to live holy, to love God and people. You find spiritual thoroughbreds in the Church.

Iron sharpens iron, and one man sharpens another.
(Proverbs 27:17 ESV)

I'm sure you've heard the African proverb, "If you want to go fast, go alone. If you want to go far, go together." [8] When you belong to a church, you'll do both: you'll go fast and go far. The Church increases your PASSION.

THE CHURCH WILL INCREASE YOUR POWER

"Though one may be overpowered, two can defend themselves. A cord of three strands is not quickly broken" (Ecclesiastes 4:12 NIV).

Remember Bob Probert, the toughest man ever in the NHL? I had a memorable game against him while playing with the Carolina Hurricanes. He was with the Chicago Blackhawks on a line with center man Doug Gilmore. Gilmore was a great player, but in the twilight of his career. He's not a very big guy at five feet ten, but he parked himself solidly in front of our team's net. It was my job as a defenseman to clear him out. I took my hockey stick and cross checked him in the back again and again. Gilmore, agitated with me, turned around and slashed me on my skates, which is unpleasant to say the least. Now I'm agitated. As I prepare to drop my gloves with Gilmore, he looks over to his winger Bob Probert and then looks back at me and calmly says, "If you touch me, he will kill you." I glanced over at Probert, who flashed a toothless grin at me. My only answer was, "You're right" and I skated away. Gilmore was no match for me on his own, but with Probert on his side, I was no match for them. As the teacher of Ecclesiastes says, "One can be overpowered but two can defend themselves!" There is strength in numbers. We are better together.

In Matthew 12, Jesus explains when a demon is cast out of a man it will look for help and return with reinforcements:

> *"Then it goes and brings with it seven other spirits more evil than itself, and they enter and dwell there, and the last state of that person is worse than the first." (Matthew 12:45 ESV)*

Sometimes I think demons are smarter than most Christians. When a demon loses a battle, it finds other stronger demons to help. When Christians struggle or fall into sin, they tend to hide or pretend everything is fine. In doing so, we rob ourselves of strength. The Church is a safe place, where we can invite others in to help us with our struggles. There is strength in numbers.

Our armed forces will occasionally put together slogans and campaigns to stir up recruits. One familiar one is the Army's *"Be all you can be."* At first the campaign was a hit, but it got stale. The Army tried a new slogan: *"Be an army of one."* It was a complete flop. Why? Because it's dumb. An army of one gets killed really quickly. They changed the slogan again, this time to, *"Army Strong."* Why? Because we are better together. [9] This isn't just true for the armed forces or a hockey team. Belonging to a church will make you stronger; it will increase your POWER.

We really are better together. *Ecclesiastes teaches us,* "A cord of three strands is not quickly broken." In other words, as we knit our lives together, we are stronger. A great picture of this is the Redwood tree. Redwoods can live for thousands of years and are the tallest trees on the planet. They can grow to heights in excess of 350 feet. That's taller than the Statue of Liberty! Surprisingly, their roots only go about ten feet deep. Where do they get their strength to grow so tall and live so long? From other Redwoods. Their roots don't go deep, but they do grow wide. Roughly 80 feet wide. Each tree's roots grow out and intertwine with the next one and the others beyond that. The trees form an unbreakable bond, giving them the strength to withstand any storm. [10] That's how the Church works. As we intertwine our lives with one another, we are stronger. We increase our POWER.

I'll close out this chapter with a quote from the "Trinity" of guy movies I mentioned earlier, *Gladiator*. Maximus and a group of ragtag prisoners are about to enter the Coliseum. Confronted with imminent death, the men are terrified. Until Maximus speaks. "Whatever comes out of these gates, we've got a better chance of survival if we work together. Do you understand? If we stay together we survive." [11] Those words ring true for the Church as well, *"If we stay together we survive."* Not only will you SURVIVE, you will THRIVE. Don't just take my word for it, let the research convince you.

-For those of you who think church is a waste of time, it's not. It actually gives you more time. In fact, almost seven years more time. A nine year study found that those who attend church regularly live an average of seven years longer than those that don't attend. [12]

-Mental health is a serious problem in the United States. A recent Harvard study revealed regular church attenders reduce their risk of depression by 30 percent. Deaths of despair are reduced by 66 percent in women and 33 percent in men. Church is great for your mental health. [13]

- Church is also great for your marriage. Another Harvard study revealed regular church attenders reduce their risk of divorce by

47 percent. You basically cut your chances of getting divorced in half! [14]

- Church is great for your kids. The same Harvard study cited the positive effects of church attendance on children, stating, "Regular service attendance helps shield children from the 'big three' dangers of adolescence: depression, substance abuse, and premature sexual activity." [15]

- The Harvard research closes with this big takeaway: "People who attended church as children are also more likely to grow up happy, to be forgiving, to have a sense of mission and purpose, and to volunteer." [16]

It sounds as if church attendance gives us power. It's one of the non-negotiables. If you want to win in life, become a regular churchgoer! I want you to win.

SECTION 3

"PLAYING TO WIN"

*Do you not know that in a race all the runners run, but only
one receives the prize? So run that you may obtain it.
(1 Corinthians 9:24 ESV)*

June 1, 2012, marks an historic date in the history of the New York Mets franchise. The Mets were at home to face their longtime rival, the St. Louis Cardinals. New York was throwing their left-handed ace, Johan Santana. St. Louis countered with their right-hander, Adam Wainwright. The Mets broke open the game in the bottom of the seventh going up 8–0. Santana was dealing. The game was in hand. Now, it was all about the possibility of a new Mets' record. Santana pitched a no-hitter through seven innings. Never before had a Mets pitcher thrown a no-hitter. Now, it was within reach.

Santana and the Mets battled their way through to the ninth inning. They made quick work of the first two batters. Only one more out to go. One batter, David Freese, stood between Santana and Mets immortality. He worked the count to 3 and 2. The anxious crowd stood to their feet as Santana prepared to deal. There's the windup and the pitch! A swing and a miss by Freese! The ecstatic crowd erupted, and the Mets dugout charged the mound to celebrate with their Ace. As player after player jumped onto one another creating this mosh pit of Mets teammates, one "player" stood out. He had a Mets team jersey on, but was also wearing jorts. (If you're unfamiliar with jorts, good for you! Jorts are jean shorts and should never be worn.)

The gentleman's name was Rafael Diaz. He was an overly zealous NY Mets fan who jumped out of the stands and onto the field in the heat of the moment. He was promptly arrested. That evening, the Mets players went out and celebrated, and Rafael Diaz went to jail. The jorts gave it away. [1] Unfortunately, I see far too many Christians wearing jorts. They wear the Christian jersey and are happy to be a fan, but they aren't actually in the game. They're at the game, but not in the game. The Apostle Paul says we are to "put on the full armor of God" (Ephesians 6:11), but instead we are often content with a jersey and jorts. God wants you in the game. He wants you to win.

PLAY TO WIN

I'll try to be as vague here as possible to protect this guy's identity, but a former teammate of mine may have been the most talented person I've ever seen lace up a pair of skates. This guy was as smooth as Gretzky and as unstoppable as Mario Lemieux...until the game started! He was what we refer to as a "practice player." He was incredible in practice, but when the game was for real, he was timid and afraid. He played not to lose, rather than to win, and so he never reached his full potential.

Jesus warns against playing not to lose. In Matthew 25, He tells The parable of the talents. In it, a wealthy man goes away on a trip, but before leaving, he entrusts a sum of money to each of his servants in order to make a profit. He gives one worker five talents, one worker two talents, and another worker one talent. (A talent was a sum of money. In today's dollars, one talent of Gold would be worth roughly 1.4 million dollars. Even if you're only a one talent guy/girl, God has entrusted you with much.) Both the five talent and two talent guys immediately went to work. They both doubled what was entrusted to them. They played to win. Listen to the Master's response:

"His master said to him, 'Well done, good and faithful servant. You have been faithful over a little; I will set you over much. Enter into the joy of your master.'" (Matthew 25:23 ESV)

The worker with one talent, however, played not to lose. He simply buried the money in the ground. When the Master returned, the one talent guy returned the one talent to his master. He made no profit. He made no difference. He played not to lose. Notice the Master's response:

"But his master answered him, 'You <u>wicked and slothful</u> servant! You knew that I reap where I have not sown and gather where I scattered no seed? Then you ought to have invested my money with the bankers, and at my coming I should have received what was my own with interest.' . . . And cast the worthless servant into the outer darkness. In that place there will be weeping and gnashing of teeth." (Matthew 25:26-27, 30 ESV)

Strong words from the Master. God has entrusted you with so much. Are you playing to win or playing not to lose?

PLAY YOUR PART

Rafael Diaz may have had a jersey, but he didn't have a role on the team. YOU have a role to play on God's team and in God's story. God saves you for a purpose:

For by grace you have been saved through faith. And this is not your own doing; it is the gift of God, not a result of works, so that no one may boast. For we are his workmanship, created in Christ Jesus for good works, which God prepared beforehand, that we should walk in them. (Ephesians 2:8-10 ESV)

Do you know your role on God's team? He has good works for you to walk in. You play a part in God's story. Don't miss your role.

Did you know that Will Smith was originally to play Neo in the hit film *The Matrix*? He turned down the role, and so it went to Keanu Reeves. Al Pacino was offered the role of Han Solo in the *Star Wars* trilogy, but turned it down. The role went to Harrison Ford. John Travolta was originally cast to play Forrest Gump. He also passed on the role, which he says is one of his biggest regrets. Tom Hanks would take the role and the Oscar. [2]

Several people throughout the Bible passed on their roles in God's story. Judas was one of the original twelve disciples, but he forfeited his role and his soul for thirty pieces of silver (Matthew 26:15). Similarly, we should be worshiping the God of Abraham, Isaac and Esau. Instead, we worship the God of Abraham, Isaac, and Jacob. Esau sold his role and soul for a bowl of stew (Genesis 25:30-33).

Ronald Wayne was one of the original founders of Apple. He owned a 10 percent stake in the start-up computer company and promptly sold it back to co-owners Steve Jobs and Steve Wozniak for $800. Today, that 10 percent share is worth ninety-five billion dollars. Can you say "regret"? But I bet you his regret pales in comparison to this man simply known as "the Rich Young Ruler." We read about him in the gospels of Matthew, Mark, and Luke. His question for Jesus was a simple one: "How can I find eternal life?" After much back and forth, Jesus replied:

"If you would be perfect, go, sell what you possess and give to the poor, and you will have treasure in heaven; and come, follow me." (Matthew 19:21 ESV)

To be clear, Jesus isn't against you having money. He's against money having you. This wealthy, young man's identity was tied to his wallet. The offer on the table is eternal life, treasures in heaven, and a seat at the table with Jesus. He most likely would have filled the void left by Judas. Here was his response:

"When the young man heard this he went away sorrowful, for he had great possessions." (Matthew 19:22 ESV)

He passed on his role in God's story. Several thousand years later he's no longer rich, he's no longer young and he's no longer a ruler. He missed the chance of a lifetime. I don't want you to miss yours. I want you to win.

In section 3, "Playing to Win," we will look at how to play a winning game in four chapters. Chapter 9, "How to Play the Game," will illustrate the importance of love for God and for others. Chapter 10, "One Shift at a Time," will examine faith and repentance. In chapter 11, "Crowd Noise," we'll consider the need for God's reassurance and "applause," and in chapter 12, I'll share some ideas about how to "Make Your Last Game Your Best."

CHAPTER 9

"HOW TO PLAY THE GAME" (LOVE GOD AND LOVE PEOPLE)

Looking back in the rear-view mirror of my life, I recall one conversation with my junior hockey coach that truly impacted me. His name was Bert Templeton. I had a love-hate relationship with Coach. I hated him, because *he demanded so much from me* and I loved him, because *he demanded so much from me.* After practice one day, he pulled me aside and asked me a simple question, "Do you want to play in the NHL?" I remember thinking, "Do I really need to answer that question? Of course I do!" He said, "If you want to play in the NHL, you have to do ONE thing better than anyone else." I immediately started taking inventory of my abilities as a hockey player: Am I the best skater, NO. The best puck handler, NO. The best offensively, NO. The best defensively, NO. Panic started to set in. I didn't do any one thing better than anyone else! And then it hit me, I was pretty good at everything. That would be my ONE thing! Who would have guessed being average in all aspects of the game (a fifty-six, remember?) could carve out a fourteen-year NHL career? But it did. It was my ONE thing. What's your ONE thing?

In Matthew 22, Jesus defines our ONE thing. There were 613 Jewish laws to observe in the Old Testament: 365 negative commands, "Thou shall nots," and 248 positive commands, "Thou shalls." When asked which was the greatest commandment, Jesus boiled it all down to ONE thing:

"Teacher, which is the great commandment in the Law?" And he said to him, "You shall love the Lord your God with all your heart and with all your soul and with all your mind. This is the great and first commandment. And a second is like it: You shall love your neighbor as yourself. On these two commandments depend all the Law and the Prophets." (Matthew 22:36-40 ESV)

Basically, Jesus boils down the entire Bible to ONE thing, love. It's our ONE thing. Loving God and loving people is the Christian's superpower that we can use to win in life.

The Apostle Paul loved the church in Philippi. He "birthed" it through much pain and suffering and desperately wanted to see this church thrive. Look at how Paul prays:

And it is my prayer that your love may abound more and more. (Philippians 1:9 ESV)

Isn't that interesting? He doesn't pray that their theology would abound more and more. He doesn't pray that their Bible reading or prayer time would abound more and more. He prays that their love would abound more and more. Paul knew, if you get the love part right, everything else will fall into place. If you get the love part right, then Bible reading, prayer, obedience will result from the overflow of that love. It's the ONE thing that impacts EVERYTHING.

LOVE GOD

"Love God and do whatever you please: for the soul trained in love to God will do nothing to offend the One who is Beloved."
—St. Augustine [1]

Over the span of my hockey career, I've been blessed to play for my country five times. It's hard to express the thrill and honor of wearing the red, white, and blue with the USA team logo. As a seventeen-year-old kid, I was invited to Colorado Springs to try out for the USA seventeen and under team. (It's like a precursor to the Olympics.) I really, really wanted to make this team. The best young athletes from around the country were competing. Little did I know, years later, several of these players would be elected into the hockey Hall of Fame. As a young Christian I was on my very best behavior, not because I was holy or anything. I just wanted God to bless me and to make the team. Every morning, I was up early reading my Bible. I spent time in prayer. I didn't cuss…much. I played well, and after three days of intense competition, the final roster was revealed. The players gathered around the locker room bulletin board and frantically searched to see if their name was on the list. I can't explain the mixture of elation and relief as I found my name. Glory to God, I made the team!

My heart was filled with gratitude for making the team, and then I went out and did what any good Christian would do after God graciously answered his prayers. I went out and got hammered drunk with my teammates. I'm not proud of that moment, but it did impact the rest of my life. As we jumped from bar to bar in Colorado Springs, a divine collision was on the horizon.

At roughly one o'clock in the morning, [1:00 a.m.,] we were greeted on a street corner by an evangelist. "Do you know Jesus Christ?" He asked my teammates and I. The guys responded with a "Whatever, dude," and moved on to the next drinking establishment. For me, those words stopped me dead in my tracks.

"Do you know Jesus Christ?" The question haunted me. Talk about a buzzkill. Instantly, a soberness came to my mind and a heaviness to my heart. I took a seat by myself on the curb, but I wasn't alone. The Lord was so real and so near to me.

He spoke to me. It wasn't audible, but it was clear. He was drawing a line in the sand for me. He said, "Adam, do you want to use *Me* for stuff or do you want to love *Me* for Me?" That night was a game changer. I realized in that moment, I wanted the Lord more than I wanted the stuff He could give me. I got it. Jesus wasn't simply a means to an end, He was the end. Jesus went from being *useful to being beautiful.*

Elisabeth Elliot, in her book *These Strange Ashes: Is God Still In Charge?*, shares an apocryphal story of Jesus and His disciples. Jesus asks His disciples, "Will you carry a stone for Me?" The disciples agree. Peter picks up the smallest stone he can find, puts it in his pocket, and follows Jesus. After some time, Jesus tells them to stop, sit down, and take out their stones. Jesus changes the stones into bread, and they all eat. That day Peter's small stone provided a short-lived lunch. The following day, Jesus again asks His disciples, "Will you carry a stone for me?" Peter this time searches for the largest stone he could possibly carry. Immediately Jesus commands, "Follow Me." Peter struggles carrying the enormous stone. After some time, the Lord again says, "Throw down your stones." Peter, expecting a super-sized loaf of bread to appear, is shocked to see only his stone. Nothing happened. Jesus begins to walk again and says, "Follow Me." Peter doesn't move. He glances down at the stone and back up at Jesus. He's confused. What happened to lunch? The Lord looks back at the puzzled disciple and simply asks, "Who were you carrying the stone for?" [2]

Who are YOU carrying the stone for? Do you do things out of LOVE for God or simply to receive things from Him? Do you LOVE God, or are your reasons for walking with him self-serving and superficial? In answering this questions we might compare our relationship with God to marriage.

My wife Susan and I have been married for thirty-five years now. We met in high school. She was the hottest girl in the entire senior class. I'm not just saying that, it was an objective fact. I couldn't believe she'd go out with me. After our first date, she said she knew we would one day be married. I wish she had told me. I was a nervous wreck the entire time dating, wondering if she was going to dump me. Here is a fact I'm not proud of, but it's true. I started dating Susan because she was hot. I didn't care much about her soul, her dreams, her hopes. I just liked the way she looked. That's OK at the beginning of a relationship, but it sure can't sustain one. Especially not for thirty-five years.

Over time, I got to know her, her personality, her likes and dislikes, her soul. Our friendship grew and our relationship deepened. These are the things that have sustained us all this time.

I remember the first time I repented of my sin and asked Jesus into my heart. I was eleven years old and the preacher had just finished a "Turn or Burn" message. The message was basically, "Do you want to burn in hell or go to heaven with Jesus?" Even as an eleven-year-old, the answer seemed fairly obvious… "I'll take Jesus, please." I wanted "fire insurance." I just didn't want to go to hell. I think that's an OK place to start. You just can't remain there. And I didn't. Like my relationship with Susan, I started cultivating a relationship with the Lord that over time has grown and grown. Heaven isn't a place for those afraid of hell, it's a place for those who love God. Do you *love* God?

In Revelation 2, Jesus warns the church at Ephesus to continue to cultivate their love for God:

"But I have this against you, that you have abandoned the love you had at first. Remember therefore from where you have fallen; repent, and do the works you did at first. If not, I will come to you and remove your lampstand from its place, unless you repent."
(Revelation 2:4-5 ESV)

Notice, there are things you can do in order to keep love vibrant and alive. Unfortunately for us today, when we hear the word "love," we think of a feeling. Feelings are great, but can be random. They come and go. The word used here for love is the Greek word "agapē." This word designates a more robust form of love. It's not primarily a feeling. It's a choice, a decisive love of the will. I can't make myself *feel* something, but I can make myself do something. There are certain things you can do as an act of your will that will cultivate love in your heart. Jesus says to the church at Ephesus, *"Do the works you did at first."* I'll refer to those works as the "care label" for your heart.

You know what the "care label" is on your clothing, right? It's that little tag that lets you know how the garment is to be handled and cleaned. The care label was a revelation to me. I'm a dude and, historically, I just chucked all my clothes in the washer regardless of color or materials. It seemed to work for gym clothes and sweatpants. I'd discover later, that's not true for cashmere.

My wife was working late. I thought I'd be the incredible husband that I am and do the laundry for her. True to form, I crammed all the clothes into the washer, dumped in some detergent, and hit "Start." Thirty minutes later, I threw the whole load in the dryer and voila! No more laundry. I was sure when my wife got home and saw the laundry finished, I'd get a sloppy wet kiss or something. When she got home, she went downstairs, and I eagerly waited for her to scream with delight. She screamed....but not with delight. *"Honey, get down here please!"* The tone didn't quite fit the sweet words. I knew I was in trouble. I walked downstairs to see her holding a miniature yellow sweater. It looked as if it belonged to "Tickle-Me Elmo." "What is this?" she inquired as if I were a three-year-old. "It's a sweater," I replied. "No, it's a cashmere sweater and can't be put in the dryer!" "How was I supposed to know that?" "Didn't you read the care label?" That day, I learned about the importance of reading the care label. Whether you know it or not, your heart has one, too.

In section 2 we went over "Training to Win." If you want to win in the Christian life, there are certain nonnegotiables. Things like reading your Bible daily, spending time in prayer, and belonging to the Church are all on the "Care Label" for your heart. We don't do these things so that God will love us. He's already displayed His eternal love for us in the cross. We do those things in order to stir our love and affection for Him. Observing the care label positions us for the Holy Spirit to do something miraculous in our hearts:

God's love has been poured into our hearts through the Holy Spirit who has been given to us. (Romans 5:5 ESV)

A deep and abiding love for God is poured into our heart by the Holy Spirit. This love is the ONE thing that will empower EVERYTHING in your life.

LOVE FOR PEOPLE

If anyone says, "I love God," and hates his brother, he is a liar; for he who does not love his brother whom he has seen cannot love God whom he has not seen. (1 John 4:20 ESV)

Some people are hard to love. Forgive me if that's too honest, but it's true. We all have people in our lives who get on our nerves, right? We all know people who we just plain don't like, correct? Did I just hear a universal "AMEN"? Then what are we to do? God provides the answer when he commands us to love people.

Pastor Ben Stuart shares an experience that illustrates this conundrum well. He and his young daughter were playing in her room. When playtime was over, he announced, "It's time to clean up your room." To which his daughter adorably responded, *"I can't want to!"* That sentiment totally resonates with me! Jesus says we are to love people…. *"I can't want to!"* Jesus tells us to love our enemies…. *"I can't want to!*" He tells us to pray for those who persecute you.... "I can't want to!" I need Jesus to change my "can't want to" so that "I want to!"

Remember, "agapē" love is not primarily a feeling, it's a decision. When I decide to obey Jesus and love unlovable people, something miraculous happens. My "want to" starts to change. God gives me a "new heart."

A NEW HEART

I had just finished a pregame chapel for the New York Jets. One of the players, Konrad Reuland, a tight end we'd recently signed, stayed afterwards for prayer. He was a mountain of a man, good-looking and full of life. We prayed that night. It was the last time I would ever see him. He finished that season with the Jets and signed the following year with the Indianapolis Colts. He finally finished his career with the Baltimore Ravens. I was absolutely stunned when I heard the news of Konrad's sudden death. He was diagnosed with a brain aneurysm that would prove fatal. He was only twenty-nine years old.

Here is where the story takes an unexpected turn. Hall of Fame baseball player Rod Carew battled numerous ailments as he aged. Among other problems, the former baseball star needed a new heart. His name went on the organ transplant list, and he waited. Finally the call came in. There was a match for Carew, a new heart. And this heart had once belonged to Konrad Reuland. The operation was a success, Carew recovered. When Konrad's mother visited Carew after her son's heart was placed into his chest, she put on a stethoscope and leaned in to hear her son's beating heart. Each heart has its own unique rhythm, no two hearts beat exactly the same way. With each beat in Carew's chest, her eyes welled up with tears. She finally broke down, "It's him....it's his heartbeat." [3]

When we obey God and choose to love people, God goes to work on our hearts. He changes our "can't want to" so that we "want to." He replaces each imperfect, ailing heart with a new one.

> *"And I will give you a new heart, and a new spirit I will put within you. And I will remove the heart of stone from your flesh and give you a heart of flesh." (Ezekiel 36:26 ESV)*

We get a new heart! A heart like Jesus. We begin to love what He loves and hate what He hates. Jesus loves people, even the most unlovable people you can imagine, and gives us the power to do the same.

Author and Christian apologist Josh McDowell grew up in a violent, dysfunctional home. His dad was the town drunk and a violent one at that. As a young boy, Josh would often come home to find his mother bloodied and beaten behind the barn. Hatred towards his father raged in his young heart. Finally, still a child, he made an oath to himself: When he was old enough and strong enough, he was going to kill his father. Something unexpected happened along the road toward premeditated murder. McDowell went off to college and had an encounter with Jesus. This hard-hearted young man became a Christian. It wasn't instantaneous or overnight, but the change was real. The rage in Josh's heart was slowly fading away almost without him knowing.

After several months, Josh asked his father to meet him for coffee. He wanted to rip into his old man and tell him how much he hated him. Instead, as he sat across the table from his dad, he opened his mouth and confessed, "Dad, I want you to know I love you." McDowell readily admits that he didn't know who was more surprised, himself or his dad. Both were stunned, but those words would prove transformative in his father's heart.

A short time afterwards, Josh was in a bad car accident. As he lay in his hospital bed, he rolled over and noticed someone in the doorway of his room. How long this person had been standing and staring at him he didn't know. But he knew immediately that the person was his dad. His father finally broke the silence and asked his son, "How can you love a man like me?" Josh candidly replied, "Dad, six months ago, I hated you. I despised you. But I came to one conclusion intellectually. God became man, His name is Jesus. And He is passionate about a relationship with you." His father prayed with his son that very moment in the hospital. His dad went from being the town drunk to the town evangelist. This is the transformative power God gives us to love unlovable people. This is the power of a new heart. [4]

TOWEL POWER

Dear children, let us not love with words or speech but with actions and in truth. (1 John 3:18 NIV)

I had the privilege to play for Hall of Fame Coach Roger Nielson. He had a brilliant hockey mind and was a genuinely kind man. He loved Jesus and the game of hockey, in that order. Outside the Vancouver Canucks arena stands a bronze statue of Roger Neilson waving a hockey stick draped with a towel. The story behind the statue is fascinating.

The Longest Game

Back in 1982, Roger was behind the bench coaching the Vancouver Canucks. The team had a below average regular season, but then seemed to find their stride once the playoffs began. Winning series after series, they suddenly found themselves in the Conference Finals facing the heavily favored Chicago Blackhawks. Vancouver took game one in dramatic fashion with a double overtime win. Game two is where our story starts to take shape. Roger and the Canucks were down 3–1 midway through the contest. The officiating seemed to be tilted towards the hometown Blackhawks. Bad call, after bad call, was killing any chance Vancouver had of getting back into the game. Finally, Roger's frustration boiled over. He grabbed one of his player's hockey sticks, attached a white towel to the end of it and started to wave it back and forth in surrender. The scene was both comical and powerful. Roger Nielson was ejected from the game and promptly fined $1,000. Vancouver lost their coach and the game, but they gained something powerful in return, the hearts of the Canucks fans.

The team landed in Vancouver late that night from Chicago. They expected to arrive home to a deserted airport. Instead, they arrived home to a sea of white towels being waved in the air. The following night when Vancouver played in front of their home crowd, every fan in attendance came armed with a towel. It was no longer a sign of surrender; it was a symbol of revolution! "Towel Power!" fueled the team and the city. Vancouver defeated Chicago and went on to compete in their first ever Stanley Cup Final. Towel Power propelled them to victory. [5] The small action of one man, Roger Neilson, started a movement.

Jesus, shortly before going to the cross, gathered His disciples together and gave them an example to follow:

Jesus, knowing that the Father had given all things into his hands, and that he had come from God and was going back to God, rose from supper. He laid aside his outer garments, and taking a towel, tied it around his waist. Then he poured water into a basin and began to wash the disciples' feet and to wipe them with the towel that was wrapped around him . . . When he had washed their feet and put on his outer garments and resumed his place, he said to them, "Do you understand what I have done to you? You call me Teacher and Lord, and you are right, for so I am. If I then, your Lord and Teacher, have washed your feet, you also ought to wash one another's feet. For I have given you an example, that you also should do just as I have done to you." (John 13:3-5,12-15 ESV)

At that time, foot washing was reserved for the most lowly of servants. Yet Jesus stooped down, humbled himself and washed their feet. It was love in action. His example started a revolution of love. Towel Power.

Pastor and author John Ortberg masterfully lays out how Jesus' example started a revolution of love in action. In his book, *Who Is This Man?: The Unpredictable Impact Of The Inescapable Jesus,* [6] Ortberg notes:

"Sociologist Rodney Stark argued that one of the primary reasons for the spread of Jesus' movement was the way his followers responded to sick people."

In 165 AD, smallpox had wiped out one-third of the population. The infected were left to die in isolation. Acting with humility and love, a small group of Jesus' followers decided to take up their towels and care for the sick.

Dionysius, a third-century bishop of Alexandria, wrote about their actions during the plagues, "Heedless of the danger, they took charge of the sick, attending to their every need, and ministering to them in Christ."

Leprosy was also considered a death sentence, and victims would be cut off from society and left to die a slow painful death all alone. Gregory of Nyssa, picked up his towel and decided to wash feet:

"Lepers have been made in the image of God. In the same way you and I have, and perhaps preserve that image better than we, let us take care of Christ while there is still time. Let us minister to Christ's needs. Let us give Christ nourishment. Let us clothe Christ. Let us gather Christ in. Let us show Christ honor."

A gathering of Christ's followers took up their towels in 325 AD and declared at the Council of Nicaea, "Wherever a cathedral existed, there must be a hospice, a place of caring for the sick and poor."

A young woman named Agnes was heartbroken when she saw the poor and suffering in Calcutta. She picked up her towel and served the poorest of the poor. We know her today as Mother Teresa.

William Wilberforce was outraged with the slave trade. He believed that all people were image bearers of God and worthy of infinite value and dignity. What could he possibly do to make a difference? Pick up his towel. It took a lifetime of humility and service, but eventually he witnessed the abolition of the slave trade in Britain.

The revolution continues today with institutions like The Salvation Army, The Red Cross, World Vision, and Compassion International, all of which began when a few individuals followed the example set by Jesus some 2,000 years ago. He picked up a towel and washed feet. Towel Power is the name of the game, and it's how you win in life. I want you to WIN.

CHAPTER 10

"ONE SHIFT AT A TIME" (FAITH AND REPENTANCE)

Jesus said to him, "Get up, take up your bed, and walk."
(John 5:8 ESV)

My dad was my first hockey coach. It was a good thing, because I wasn't very talented. I probably shouldn't even have made the team, but when your Old Man is the coach, I guess you gotta make the team, right? I mean, you can't cut your kid! I remember asking him about those early years. He told me, "You were a terrible skater!" I thought to myself, "Thanks, Dad!" He went on to say, "You fell down a lot....but *you always got right back up.*" Honestly, that's the secret to winning in Christianity and life itself. Whoever GETS UP the most wins.

Mistakes and failures are part of sports and part of life. The very best athletes of all time failed tremendously, but they learned to get back up again. Babe Ruth held the home run record (714) for decades, but did you know he also held the strikeout record as well? He struck out 1,330 times! [1] That kind of performance requires a lot of

"Getting Up"! Ruth's motto: "Never allow the fear of striking out keep you from playing the game!" [2]

Ty Cobb holds the all-time batting average record at .366. [3] If you're doing the math, that means he failed to get a hit almost 6.5 times out of 10. That's a lot of failure to deal with, and he's considered the very best!

Michael Jordan, the "G.O.A.T.", failed a bunch as well. He says it's how he became the "<u>G</u>reatest <u>O</u>f <u>A</u>ll <u>T</u>ime." *"I've missed more than 9,000 shots in my career. I've lost almost 300 games. 26 times, I've been trusted to take the game winning shot and missed. I've failed over and over and over again in my life. And that is why I succeed."* [4] It sounds like he learned to "Get Up."

It's not only athletes who fail. All the icons in human history deserved a PhD in getting up. It was failure after failure and learning to pick themselves back up again that made their success. Walt Disney was fired from his job at a local newspaper because he "lacked creativity." Thomas Edison invented the lightbulb, but not before failing 2,774 times! Steve Jobs was fired from Apple, the very company he helped found. If he hadn't gotten up, we wouldn't have the iPhone. Harry Potter novels have grossed an estimated 7.7 billion dollars. Author and creator J.K. Rowling was turned down by twelve different publishing companies before finally being accepted. All of these icons went on to do amazing things, but not before learning to "Get Up." [5]

The Bible is filled with flawed men and women. The great "prophet" Homer Simpson had this revelation as he set down his Bible, "All these people are a mess ....except this one guy (Jesus)." Many, if not all, of the heroes of the Christian faith had epic fails! Moses, David, Abraham, all of them sinned horribly. Clearly, they weren't perfect people. They were just great at getting up.

The Apostle Peter's failure was not just epic, it was personal. On the night of the Last Supper, Jesus sat with His disciples and broke bread. That night, Jesus explained to Peter, "Tonight, you will deny me three times before the rooster crows." Peter vehemently denied it, and they headed off to the Garden of Gethsemane to pray. Soon afterwards, Jesus is arrested and all the disciples scatter. Peter follows from a distance. Jesus is beaten, bloodied, and mocked as He is transported across the temple courtyard. Peter, warming himself by a fire, is accused of knowing Jesus:

> *Then a servant girl, seeing him as he sat in the light and looking closely at him, said, "This man also was with him." But he denied it, saying, "Woman, I do not know him." And a little later someone else saw him and said, "You also are one of them." But Peter said, "Man, I am not." And after an interval of about an hour still another insisted, saying, "Certainly this man also was with him, for he too is a Galilean." But Peter said, "Man, I do not know what you are talking about." And immediately, while he was still speaking, the rooster crowed. And the Lord turned and looked at Peter. And Peter remembered the saying of the Lord, how he had said to him, "Before the rooster crows today, you will deny me three times." And he went out and wept bitterly. (Luke 22:56-62 ESV)*

See what I mean by epic and personal? Honestly, I don't know how you recover from that one. Have you ever been there before? I know I have. I've experienced those moments in life when you ask yourself, *"How could I?"* Or, *"I can't believe I did that."* You go from a sense of overwhelming guilt to a crushing shame. It's no longer what you <u>did</u> was wrong. Now, <u>you're</u> wrong. Peter felt the crushing weight of sin and shame. He would go on to do great things for God, but not before learning to Get Up. The Apostle Paul compares our life to a fight, the fight of faith:

> *Fight the good fight of the faith. Take hold of the eternal life to which you were called and about which you made the good confession in the presence of many witnesses.*
> *(1 Timothy 6:12 ESV)*

Guilt and shame will knock you out of the game of life if you don't fight back. Your failures don't get to define you. Jesus does! As long as you Get Up and learn to fight one more round.

"Gentleman" Jim Corbett would become the Heavy-Weight Champion of the world on September 7, 1892. He knocked out the seemingly invincible former champion John Sullivan in the 21st ROUND! That's not a typo. They fought for 21 rounds! Today a sanctioned boxing match is just 12 rounds. The 21-round match must have felt like a walk in the park compared to the 61-round match he fought against Peter Jackson [6]. Corbett wrote a famous description that encapsulates the art of Getting Up:

> "Fight one more round. When your feet are so tired that you have to shuffle back to the center of the ring, fight one more round. When your arms are so tired that you can hardly lift your hands to come on guard, fight one more round. When your nose is bleeding and your eyes are black and you are so tired you wish your opponent would crack you one on the jaw and put you to sleep, fight one more round—remembering that the man who always fights one more round is never whipped." [7]

The Apostle Peter decided to fight one more round. He'd go on to do great things! He preached the first sermon on the day of Pentecost and 3,000 people came to Christ. He led the Early Church and even raised a little girl from the dead. None of that would have happened if he hadn't gotten up to fight one more round. Get up! It's how Peter won in life and how you will too. Whoever gets up the most wins!

FORGETTING AND STRAINING

Most Christians are being crucified on a cross between two thieves: Yesterday's regret and tomorrow's worries.
—*Warren W. Wiersbe [8]*

It became known simply as the "Monday Night Massacre." The New England Patriots were playing host to the New York Jets week thirteen of the 2010 NFL season. Despite the fact I am a Christian, I detest the Patriots, not as individuals but as an organization. They are "The Evil Empire." I don't think you can be a Christian and root for them. I'm joking! (But it's true.) We were having a strong season going 9-2 up until this point and undefeated on the road. All that was about to change. New England destroyed us 45-3 in front of their home crowd along with the millions that watched on Monday Night Football. It was humiliating.

The following day, rather than ripping into his players, Coach Rex Ryan took a different approach. He assembled his team outside the practice facility and had them gather around a large hole dug in the ground. He took a game ball from the massacre the previous night and the funeral service began. Rex announced, "We're burying this game and all that happened Monday night." [9] The players agreed and said "AMEN." The ball was buried in the ground along with the memory of that embarrassing loss. Just five short weeks later, the Jets faced the Patriots once again, this time in the Divisional Championship Game. That night, we destroyed Bill Belichick and the "Evil Empire" 28-21 and advanced to the AFC Championship game.

Burying past failures and mistakes is essential to winning in life. The Apostle Paul, for instance, did some incredible things. He wrote two-thirds of the letters found in the New Testament. The Bible mentions he went to the "third heaven" (2 Corinthians 12:2). I'm not even exactly sure what that means, but it must have been awesome. His handkerchief healed sick folks, and he even raised a guy from the dead. His was a truly remarkable life, but none of it would have happened if he hadn't learned to bury past failures.

Have things from your past ever haunted you, things you did or said that you just can't seem to shake? Like most of us, Paul had a past. Prior to his conversion to Christianity, he was known as Saul, and he violently and relentlessly persecuted the Church. He had seen and done some things that you just can't unsee and undo. For example, he was an accomplice to the murder of Stephen, the Church's first martyr. Stephen died a slow and painful death by way of stoning. Have you ever seen someone struck by an object with velocity behind it? While playing for Atlanta, an opposing player took a slapshot that struck me in the face. A slapshot can exceed speeds of 100 mph. When it hit me, the blow crushed the entire right side of my face. I couldn't stop the bleeding, and blood poured out from my face onto the ice. The 19,000 fans in attendance all gasped and looked away in horror. That was simply one puck striking a man. Stephen was stoned repeatedly. Blow after bloody blow. And Paul liked it. In fact, he held the jackets of the murderous mob so he could watch. You can't unsee something like that. How would he shake this event and many others like it? He did it by taking a page out of Coach Rex Ryan's playbook and burying his past in order to move forward.

> *Brothers, I do not consider that I have made it my own. But one thing I do: forgetting what lies behind and straining forward to what lies ahead, I press on toward the goal for the prize of the upward call of God in Christ Jesus.*
> (Philippians 3:13-14 ESV)

FORGETTING WHAT'S BEHIND

I'm a bit of a "gym rat." I've always loved the gym and everything it has to offer. After spending hours, years, in the gym, I can always tell when someone has never been before. They will use the equipment wrong or violate gym etiquette. I recall one time an older gentleman who was new to the gym jumped onto the treadmill near me. He started with a slow walking pace, but soon picked it up to a brisk jog. He was struggling to watch the TV screens on the wall while simultaneously remaining on the treadmill. He looked like someone texting and driving. Figuratively speaking, he was all over the road. Finally, it happened. He missed the tread and started to fall. I say started to fall, because he grabbed the handle on the front of the treadmill as his legs shot off the back of the machine. Now, with his hands firmly gripped onto the front handle, his shins were being sandpapered off by the fast-moving tread. You could smell the flesh burning off his legs! One by one, the onlooking gym members yelled, "Let go! Just let go!" The man did let go, but only with one hand. The other was still firmly attached to the handle. In essence, all he did was rotate his body so that a fresh portion of skin would be rubbed off. He was making it worse! Again gym members screamed, "Let go!" His response was to alternate hands which again rotated his body. If the goal was to burn the skin off his shins entirely, he was succeeding. One last time, gym members pleaded, "Let go, you're hurting yourself!" Finally, he let go. The treadmill shot him out like a waterslide. He hit the ground, dusted himself off, and jumped back on the treadmill as if nothing had ever happened. It was priceless. And I just described many of you. Not letting go of failures and mistakes from the past will only harm your present. I'll repeat the sage advice from the gym, "Let go, you're hurting yourself!"

As a player, I was terrible at letting go. Coaches always encouraged me to have a "short-term" memory. Don't allow one bad shift or one bad game to impact the next one. I stunk at moving on. Rather than *learning* from my past, I decided to live there. I couldn't let it go, even though dwelling on my past destroyed my present.

Forgetting is hard, isn't it? I mean how do you make yourself forget something? This is where the words of Paul help us. When he says, "forgetting what's behind", the word "forgetting" in the original Greek literally means "to neglect." I can do that! I'm really good at neglecting stuff. If I neglect plants and don't water them, eventually they wither and die. If I neglect relationships and don't nurture them, eventually they wither and die. If I neglect my body and don't take care of it, eventually it will wither and die. It works the same way with your past mistakes and failures. If you neglect them, eventually they will wither and die.

The starting point for neglecting our past failures and sins is "owning" them. Pastor Mark Batterson puts it this way, "We either own our past, or our past will own us." [10] The Bible calls this "confession":

If we say we have no sin, we deceive ourselves, and the truth is not in us. If we confess our sins, he is faithful and just to forgive us our sins and to cleanse us from all unrighteousness. (1 John 1:8-9 ESV)

The first step of forgetting your past is being honest with yourself and with God. Own your sin and screw-ups. What you did was stupid, wrong and sinful....and the Lord paid for it on the cross 2,000 years ago. Confess your sins to Him and allow Christ to dust you off (cleanse you of sin) and put you back into the game of life. Paul owned his sin and shame, admitting:

I was once a blasphemer and a persecutor and a violent man....
Christ Jesus came into the world to save sinners—
of whom I am the worst. (1 Timothy 1:13-15 NIV)

Paul owns his past sin and shame, but he doesn't live there. Rather than dwelling on his failures and faults, he allows the reality of Christ's work on the cross to get him back in the game of life. Now, instead of being crushed under the weight of regret and shame, Paul is filled with gratitude and worship:

But I received mercy for this reason, that in me, as the foremost, Jesus Christ might display his perfect patience as an example to those who were to believe in him for eternal life. To the King of the ages, immortal, invisible, the only God, be honor and glory forever and ever. Amen. (1 Timothy 1:16-17 ESV)

FORGETTING AND FORGIVING

"Every one says forgiveness is a lovely idea, until they have something to forgive." —C.S. Lewis [11]

Oftentimes forgetting will look and feel an awful lot like forgiving. We live in a broken world full of hurting people. And hurting people hurt people. None of us gets out of the game of life without being wounded by someone.

Forgiveness can be difficult, but not to forgive, can be deadly! Author and professor Lewis B. Smedes says, "To forgive is to set a prisoner free and discover that the prisoner was you." [12]

I could point you to volumes of medical research showing how bitterness and resentment flood the body with cortisol and stress. In fact, the very term *resentment* means "to feel it again." By hanging onto unforgiveness, we literally replay the trauma perpetrated against us. We actually harm ourselves over and over again. As a pastor for more than twenty years, I've watched unforgiveness slowly eat away at the life and vitality of people. It's like a cancer to the soul. God wants you free and so do I.

It may help you to loosen your grip on unforgiveness, when you realize what forgiveness is NOT:

- Forgiveness doesn't mean what was done to you was OK or no big deal. It was sin, and it was wrong.

- Forgiveness doesn't mean that there aren't consequences for sin. If someone commits a crime, they can be forgiven, but they are still going to jail.

- Forgiveness doesn't necessarily mean reconciliation. You can forgive someone, but also maintain healthy boundaries and distance. Sometimes these are necessary.

The Apostle Peter once asked Jesus, how many times he needed to forgive his brother? Seven times, would that be enough? Jesus' answer was shocking and spot-on:

> *Jesus said to him, "I do not say to you seven times, but seventy-seven times." (Matthew 18:22 ESV)*

If you've ever tried to forgive someone who has really hurt you, you know it can feel like it takes seventy-seven times! We've all had those moments when we forgive someone and, just when we thought it was behind us, something happens and unforgiveness bubbles up again. We may need to forgive over and over again, but eventually the *"bell will stop ringing."*

Corrie Ten Boom was a Holocaust survivor, but her survival came at great cost. She watched her family and fellow Jews suffer and die at the hands of the Nazis. She could have held on to bitterness and unforgiveness for the remainder of her life. Instead, she chose forgiveness and freedom. How did she get there? How could she ever forgive such atrocities? She said she stopped "pulling on the rope." Perhaps you've seen an old church building with a massive bell in the steeple. When you pull the bell's rope, it violently swings side to side, delivering the loud ringing noise. Once you stop pulling the rope, momentum keeps the bell ringing for a while. [13]

But eventually, over time, the bell stops swinging and stops ringing. Silence. Peace. Forgiveness. Stop pulling the rope of the past. God wants you free and so do I. I want you to win.

You can't change the past, but you can decide what to do with it. My youngest daughter is a veterinary technician. What that means is she does all the work and the vet gets all the cash. She spends most of her time helping and healing animals. But occasionally, the animal can't be helped and needs to be put down. This task, no matter how necessary, is never pleasant. Once a woman brought her sick, elderly dog in. After exhausting all options, it was determined the dog should be put down. The owner agreed and stood next to her dog as my daughter administered the necessary drugs to put the animal to sleep. The animal went quietly and peacefully to sleep then passed away without pain. The owner on the other hand, had a change of heart and started yelling, "Reverse it! Reverse it!" My daughter thought to herself, "Lady, you know it doesn't work that way. When it's done it's done. You can't reverse it." And so it is with the past. It's over. YOU CAN'T REVERSE IT. But you can NEGLECT IT. You can CONFESS IT. You can FORGIVE IT.

STRAINING TOWARDS WHAT'S AHEAD

When Paul admonishes us to "strain" he means to "reach out" to "take hold of." It's not enough to simply forget the past. We have to make the most of today and reach for tomorrow. Paul describes it in Ephesians as:

> ...*making the most of every opportunity, because the days are evil.*
> *(Ephesians 5:16 NIV)*

Are you making the most of the minutes, hours, and days God has given to you?

The Sistine Chapel is one of Michelangelo's finest works. Ironically, he hated every minute he spent working on what many consider his masterpiece. The project took four painstaking years to complete, and besides, he much preferred sculpting to painting. A rival sculptor named Bramante reportedly suggested the Pope commission Michelangelo to paint the Sistine Chapel thinking he'd do a poor job, as painting was not his strong suit. Swing and a miss! It is widely considered one of the greatest works of art of all time. The chapel's ceiling is intricately arrayed with ornate paintings illustrating the narrative of the Bible. One I'm certain you've seen before is called *The Creation of Adam*. [14]

In it you see Almighty God stressing and straining, reaching towards Adam. Adam, on the other hand, can barely extend his index finger to touch his Creator. Seriously, I want to punch Adam right in the face. He shows no passion and no zeal, just apathy and indifference. In fact, a 2022 study from Lifeway Research revealed that three-fourths of pastors believe that apathy is the primary people-dynamic challenge they face in their churches [15]. Don't fall into that trap. Heed these words from the Apostle Paul and make today your Masterpiece!

Whatever you do, work heartily, as for the Lord and not for men. (Colossians 3:23 ESV)

PASSION IN ACTION

As a young boy, Theodore was terrified to walk into church. His mother Mittie asked him why. He simply replied, that 'zeal lived there and it might eat him'. She continued, "What do you think zeal is?" To which he replied, "A dragon or alligator that will eat you." [16] His mother inquired where this idea came from. He said that the pastor read about zeal. Mittie started reading through Bible verses that spoke about zeal to her son. Finally, she landed on the one that had grabbed him. It was from John 2:

And his disciples remembered that it was written,
The zeal of thine house hath eaten me up. (John 2:17 KJV)

Zeal. It's not a word we use much anymore, nor do we see it much either. When I think of zeal, I think of "passion in action." Young Theodore grew up to be a man of passion as well as the twenty-sixth president of the United States. We witnessed zeal in action on October 14, 1912. Moments before Theodore "Teddy" Roosevelt was to give a speech, a would-be assassin shot him in the chest with a .32 caliber bullet. With the bullet firmly lodged in his chest, Roosevelt refused to go to the hospital until after he'd delivered his speech. He opened by saying, "Friends, I shall ask you to be as quiet as possible. I don't know whether you fully understand that I have just been shot. The bullet is in me now, so I cannot make a very long speech, but I will try my best." He spoke for the next ninety minutes! [17] That's zeal! That's passion in action.

Jesus was a man of zeal. So often people think Jesus was just some nice, soft-spoken guy that never raised his voice or never made a scene. The Bible paints a different picture of the Son of God. In fact, the passage from John 2:17 that sparked fear in young Theodore comes immediately after Jesus arrives in Jerusalem for Passover. Entering the Temple, he sees commerce, corruption and human greed and is moved to action.

In the temple he found those who were selling oxen and sheep and pigeons, and the money-changers sitting there. And making a whip of cords, he drove them all out of the temple, with the sheep and oxen. And he poured out the coins of the money-changers and overturned their tables. (John 2:14-15 ESV)

Jesus was a man of zeal, passion in action, and so were His disciples. In Acts 5, the apostles are arrested by the Temple guards for sharing the Good News of Jesus. Here is what happened next:

And when they had called in the apostles, they <u>beat</u> them and charged them not to speak in the name of Jesus, and let them go. Then they left the presence of the council, rejoicing that they were counted worthy to suffer dishonor for the name. (Acts 5:40-41 ESV)

As readers, we might just gloss over the word "beaten." What that means is that they were each given thirty-nine lashes with a leather whip to their bare skin. Each would receive two lashes on their back, be flipped over and given one lash to the front. They would repeat that sequence thirteen times for each disciple. And the Bible said they left REJOICING! That is passion in action. That is a zeal. Are you zealous for God? It's how we win in life, and I want you to win.

WEIGHT AND WORRY OVER TOMORROW

"Therefore do not be anxious about tomorrow, for tomorrow will be anxious for itself. Sufficient for the day is its own trouble." (Matthew 6:34 ESV)

Forgetting what's behind us can be difficult, but worry over tomorrow can be paralyzing. If you are going to win in life, you're going to have to "strain towards what's ahead." The Greek word used for "ahead" is unique. It means "what's right in front of you or before you." Paul is saying, "Be where you are." Don't be off into tomorrow, be where you are. Tomorrow is God's business. You remain faithful with today.

If you haven't seen the 2005 comedy *Hitch*, shame on you! It stars Will Smith and Kevin James. Kevin James plays a nerdy and romantically awkward guy named Albert. Albert desperately wants to win the affection of the beautiful Allegra. He seeks help from the "Love Doctor" Hitch, played by Will Smith. Albert is scheduled to join Allegra at a gala where there will be dancing. Hitch is concerned. Albert insists it will be fine, he's "got moves." Skeptical, Hitch asks to see these dance moves. Albert obliges and lets it all hang out. He does the *Cabbage Patch*, the *Pizza Roll*, and don't forget *The Q-tip*. Hitch is at a loss for words. Meanwhile, Albert thinks he just crushed it and is waiting for a high-five. Instead, he gets a slap in the face! Hitch warns Albert to NEVER perform any of those moves in public ever again. Instead, his ONE and ONLY move is to snap his fingers to the beat and toe tap left and right. That's it! Hitch demonstrates in order to drive home the point and simply repeats, *"This is where you live."* [18] And that's our move as well, be where you are. The past is in the past and tomorrow is God's business. Today is where you live. Be faithful living your best life today and trust God for your tomorrow.

Amazon recently released statistics from their most popular Kindle books. The statistics concerning the Bible reveal our deep angst about the future. Do you know what the most what highlighted verse in the Bible is according to Amazon? Here it is:

Do not be anxious about anything, but in everything by prayer and supplication with thanksgiving let your requests be made known to God. And the peace of God, which surpasses all understanding, will guard your hearts and your minds in Christ Jesus.
(Philippians 4:6-7 ESV)

Seems like fear and anxiety over tomorrow was a problem for Paul back then and for us today. The antidote for fear and anxiety is also the same today as it was then: prayer. When we feel the weight of care it is our warning signal to find peace in prayer.

In the '80s the rock group Van Halen ruled the airwaves. They sold out venues around the globe. As their fan base grew, so did their elaborate stage sets and pyrotechnics. Smoke machines, lighting, and the occasional explosion made each show increasingly more exciting for fans and more dangerous for the band. The margin for error was slim. Lead singer David Lee Roth added a clause to the contract between the venue and the band. It was known as the "M&M clause." The contract demanded that a bowl of M&M's had to be available backstage at all times. All brown M&M's had to be removed from the bowl or the contract was null and void. The M&M clause was a "trip-wire clause" [19]. The band knew if there were brown M&M's in the bowl, the venue hadn't read the contract carefully, which meant that they hadn't read the safety protocols either and the band could be in danger. God has given you a trip-wire clause. When you feel worry, fear and anxiety bubbling up in your soul, that becomes your trip wire. It's time to pray! Notice the sequence presented in the passage from Phillipians; as we release our cares to God in prayer, we receive the promise of a peace that "passes understanding." The peace of God will literally "guard" our hearts from the onslaught of fear and anxiety.

GOD'S GOT TOMORROW

Tomorrow isn't a place God wonders about. It's a place he already inhabits. That should be unbelievably comforting to you. A benevolent loving Father waits for you in tomorrow. Allow me to illustrate. Luca Manfe was a member of my church and a friend. I performed his wedding to his lovely wife, Catherine. I remember the day Luca pulled me aside after church one Sunday and let me know he would be gone for the next few months. He was taking another shot at being on *Masterchef*. He tried the previous year, in season three of the popular FOX series, but was unsuccessful. We prayed over season four and off he went to compete. Eventually, he returned home and I asked him how it went. He said he was forced to sign nondisclosure agreement and couldn't talk about it. The show is shot months in advance. The first few episodes of *Masterchef* didn't go great for Luca. He struggled with his skills and techniques through many of the early rounds, but his charisma and personality carried him through. Midway through the competition, something changed. Luca was hitting his stride and finding his groove. Eventually, he cooked his way to the grand finale! Luca rented out a local restaurant in New York City and invited his closest friends and family to watch the finale along with him on the restaurants big screen TV. The suspense that night was palpable. I was nervous and so was everyone else. Well, almost everyone. Luca was cool as can be. The suspense crescendoed as the judges' decisions were in. The room was silent, and we all leaned forward to the edge of our seats. Finally the judges announced, "And the winner of Masterchef Season Four is… Luca Manfe!" The room erupted! We couldn't believe it. But Luca could. He wasn't surprised at all. He already lived that reality. He was already there.

God is not wondering about your tomorrow either. He is already there. He's waiting for you. He has EVERYTHING you need to do ALL He's called you to do. God's got your tomorrow. Trust Him and be faithful with today.

CHECKMATE

This painting's original title was *Die Schachspieler*. It's better known in English as "Checkmate." The painting depicts a satanic looking character playing chess with a perplexed and defeated young soul. An angel looks at the young man with pity. Checkmate! The Devil wins. There have been moments in my life when I've felt like that young man. Stuck and defeated. No way out and no way forward. Checkmate! The Good News of the Gospel is that with Jesus you always have another move.

Paul Morphy, a chess phenom born in Virginia, learned to play by the age of ten and became a chess master at the ripe old age of seventeen. He traveled the world and defeated any that dared challenge him. At twenty-one he retired from competitive chess. A bit of a celebrity, Morphy was invited to the home of Reverend R.R. Harrison along with several other Virginian elites. Hanging on the wall in the good Reverend's home, was a painting that mesmerized Morphy, "Checkmate." A strange sense of sorrow for the young man in the painting gripped the chess master. After studying the painting for several minutes, Morphy blurted out, "He has another move! I can win with that board."

The stunned host obliged the chess master and replicated the painting's chess board. Morphy did indeed have another move, or rather a series of maneuvers that defeated his satanic opponent. He'd won! [20]

And that is our story. All looked lost when they put Jesus in the tomb two thousand years ago. But it wasn't, Jesus had another move. He got up out of the grave. In doing so, He defeated death and the Devil on our behalf. With Jesus, you always have another move. Remember, whoever gets up the most, wins in life. When the Devil says, "Checkmate," don't you believe it. You always have another move. *Get up. Forget what's behind and strain towards what's ahead.* It's how you win in life and I want you to win.

CHAPTER 11

"CROWD NOISE" (CHRISTIAN COURAGE AND HEAVEN'S APPLAUSE)

"If the world hates you, know that it has hated me before it hated you. If you were of the world, the world would love you as its own; but because you are not of the world, but I chose you out of the world, therefore the world hates you." (John 15:18-19 ESV)

Every athlete learns from an early age that sometimes they have to ignore crowd noise. While the cheers from fans can be inspiring and exhilarating, when the crowd turns against you, the effect can be devastating. Former NFL Quarterback Mark Brunell knows all about crowd noise. Mark is both a friend and a follower of Christ [1]. He once shared with me and a group of friends about the nightmarish 2004 season. He laughs about it now, but it was far from being funny back then. In 2004, Mark was traded from the Jacksonville Jaguars to the Washington Redskins. Expectations were high for the upcoming campaign, but things got off to a real bumpy start. The team went 3-5 through the midway point of the season. Brunell wasn't playing well, and pressure was mounting from the restless fan base. It was week eight of regular season play, and the Cincinnati Bengals were in town to take on the struggling Redskins. Mark's confidence was at an all-time low. Prior to taking the field, one of Mark's coaches pulled him aside and bluntly stated, "We need you to play well today." Thanks, Captain Obvious!

The game started strong for Mark and the Skins. He drove the team right down the field on the opening series. The fans were into it. The stadium was electric. Deep in Cincinnati territory, Mark breaks the huddle and steps under center. As he barks out the play, the fans anxiously wait. Mark drops back to pass, locks onto his receiver, and delivers the ball…to the other team! The Bengal's defender ran the interception all the way back for a touchdown. The stunned crowd was momentarily silent as the shock set in. Then the the silence was broken by disgruntled chants of *"Ram-sey, Ram-sey."* Patrick Ramsey was the backup quarterback for the Redskins. The fans were finished with Mark and demanded the backup be put in.

The chants intensified, *"Ram-sey, Ram-sey."* Louder and louder the crowd roared in unison, *"Ram-sey, Ram-sey!"* The chorus rippled upward from the lower seating straight to the luxury boxes, *"Ram-sey, Ram-sey!"* It was infectious. In fact, Mark's own sons joined in! Seated up in the luxury boxes, his three boys were too young to really understand what was happening and got caught up in the moment. They joined in at the top of their lungs, *"Ram-sey! Ram-sey!"* His own kids were inadvertently cheering for his demise. The whole world seemed to be against him. Mark Brunell was benched for the remainder of the season.

Jesus knows a thing or two about crowd noise. He knows what it feels like to have the world turn against you. In Matthew 21, we read the story of Jesus' triumphal entry into Jerusalem for Passover week. Massive crowds chanted and cheered, *"Hosanna!"* which means

'Come, Lord, save!' The chants and praise grew louder and louder, *"Hosanna to the King!"* The scene was euphoric, almost chaotic. Jewish officials feared the Roman authorities would feel threatened by shouts for a "King" and demanded that Jesus quiet the people. His response was simply, 'If they stop, the rocks will cry out.' The crowd was for Him.... until they weren't. In just a few short days, that same crowd will cry out, *"Crucify Him! Crucify Him!"*

What do you do when it feels like the world is against you? Jesus knew the answer, He looked up. He lived His life, not for the approval of men, but for the approval of His heavenly Father. He was playing the game of life for an audience of One. The chants of "Crucify Him!" were drowned out by the thunder of His Father's "Well done!" As Jesus hung on the cross, His eyes stayed locked onto His Father until the very end:

> ***Then Jesus, calling out with a loud voice, said, "Father, into your hands I commit my spirit!" And having said this he breathed his last. (Luke 23:46 ESV)***

Jesus lived for His Father and not His fans. He chose the applause of heaven over the approval of men. His performance was over, but Jesus wasn't finished. On the third day He rose from the dead triumphant and victorious. The heavens now declare Him "King of Kings" and "Lord of Lords." What a comeback story!

Speaking of a comeback story, Mark Brunell had one as well. Mark decided to look up and play for an audience of One. He didn't need to please his fans, only his heavenly Father. On the third day he rose again! OK, it wasn't the third day, it was the following season. Mark got up, dusted himself off, and led the Redskins to their first playoff berth in years and was nominated for "Comeback Player of the Year." How will you handle crowd noise? Who will you listen to? Who will you live for? The fans or the Father?

AUDIENCE OF ONE

Trust in the LORD with all your heart, and do not lean on your own understanding. In all your ways acknowledge him, and he will make straight your paths. (Proverbs 3:5-6 ESV)

I recently read the story of Dennis Wong. Dennis was a Division II collegiate football player. He rarely got on the field, but loved being part of the team. After putting together an impressive string of wins, Dennis and his teammates made it all the way to the Conference Finals. The evening before the big game, Coach was in his hotel room going over the next day's game plan. He was interrupted by a frantic knock at the door. He opened the door to find a somewhat distraught-looking Dennis. Coach asked him what was up? Dennis got right to the point. "Coach, you have to put me in tomorrow. Please, you gotta let me play!" After hearing the intensity in his voice, Coach promised he'd consider it.

Game time rolled around and the starting lineup was announced. Coach would allow Dennis to play special teams for the opening kickoff, and then he'd go back to the bench as a backup. Dennis' team kicks off, and he streaks down the field like a man on a mission. The opposition's return man fields the kick when suddenly and violently he's hit by Dennis and the ball pops loose. Dennis and his team recovered the ball! They managed a field goal and took the early lead. The plan was to sit Dennis on the bench, but after that play Coach had no choice but to keep Dennis in. That day Dennis was a force on the field and played like a man possessed. He made big play after big play. With seconds remaining in the game and the team needing a stop, who was there for the final tackle? Dennis Wong. Time expired and as the buzzer sounded the fans flooded the field. They were Conference Champions.

The celebration in the locker room went on for some time. Slowly, the euphoria died down and the players showered and left. Coach noticed one player, still in his equipment, alone in the corner sobbing. It was Dennis. Coach made his way over and inquired, "What's wrong? You just played the greatest game of your life!" Dennis gathered himself and replied, "Coach, you remember my dad, right?" "Of course! He always loved to come and listen to us practice." Dennis' father was legally blind, but he hardly ever missed a practice. With tears streaming down his face, Dennis informed his Coach, "My dad passed away last week, and this was the first time he was able to SEE me play." I'm not sure whether or not that story is true. But I am sure, if you are a Christian, it is true for you. It is *your* story. Your heavenly Father is watching you play in the game of life. You play for an audience of One.

Stephen played for an audience of One. He was the Church's first martyr and received the first ever standing ovation in the heavenly realm. We read about it in Acts 7. Stephen is proclaiming the Gospel to a crowd that would soon turn into a mob. The more he pleaded they turn to Jesus, the angrier they got. Finally, the mob picked up stones and hurled them at Stephen. With each deadly blow, life drained from his beaten body. But when he looked up, he saw Jesus standing at the right hand of God. He heard the applause of heaven and received a standing ovation from the very Son of God:

> *Now when they heard these things they were enraged, and they ground their teeth at him. But he, full of the Holy Spirit, gazed into heaven and saw the glory of God, and Jesus standing at the right hand of God. (Acts 7:54-55 ESV)*

The boos from the crowd were drowned out by the applause of heaven.

ROAD GAMES

For this world is not our permanent home; we are looking forward to a home yet to come. (Hebrews 13:14 NLT)

For any athlete, playing on the road can be extremely intimidating. Some arenas can be especially scary places to play. As a rookie, nobody warned me about playing in the old Chicago Stadium. The building was ancient. You had to climb up a flight of stairs in order to get to the ice surface. Jumping onto the ice was like jumping into the Roman Colosseum. The fans seemed to be right on top of you. In this stadium, the national anthem was not sung, it was played on an organ, the kind you see in haunted houses. As the creepy organ played, the fans cheered the entire time, making the building literally shake.

The Old Boston Garden was a scary place to play as well. My first time visiting the Old Garden, I wasn't in the lineup and was sitting up in the press box with another veteran teammate, Dean Evason. He looked over at me and said, "Kid, right now you are up here, wishing you were down there playing. Soon you will be down there playing, wishing you were back up here." He was right! It was a scary place to play.

Philly is an AMAZING sports town—for the home team! Whoever named Philadelphia, the City of Brotherly Love, obviously never played there on the visiting team! The fans are incredible; they're also nuts.

One year the Philadelphia Eagles fans threw snowballs at Santa Claus during halftime! Who does that? Eagles fans were so belligerent towards opposing teams and their fans, an actual jail cell and courtroom had to be set up inside the stadium.

The City of Brotherly Love? I'm not so sure, but they are awesome sports fans. Playing on the road is always difficult.

The Christian is no longer playing with home ice advantage. Increasingly, it's apparent we are playing on the road. There was a time when living by Christian morals and biblical principles was celebrated. Those days are long gone. Today, living an overt Christian life won't get you celebrated. It might get you canceled, marginalized, or maybe even demonized. A biblical view on sexuality will get you labeled as "repressed" or maybe even a "hater." Our views on marriage and family are viewed as outdated and uneducated. We are playing on the road. Jesus warned us:

"If the world hates you, know that it has hated me before it hated you. If you were of the world, the world would love you as its own; but because you are not of the world, but I chose you out of the world, therefore the world hates you." (John 15:18-19 ESV)

To win in the Christian life, you're going to have to decide whether you want the approval of men or the approval of God. You can't have them both.

The Apostle Paul traveled with a man named Demas, his friend and disciple. Demas worked with Paul starting churches and spreading the Gospel. Somewhere along the line, Demas felt pressure to fit into the world around him. Sadly, he sold out. He abandoned both Paul and the Gospel:

For Demas, in love with this present world, has deserted me and gone to Thessalonica. (2 Timothy 4:10 ESV)

Now, looking back through the lens of eternity, I wonder if Demas would want a do-over. The approval of people over the applause of heaven is a crappy trade. By the way, the name Demas means "popular." You're going to have to decide whether you want to be popular with God or popular with people.

Popular opinion kept an entire generation out of the Promised Land. In Numbers 13, Moses sends out twelve spies to scout out the Promised Land. After several days the spies return with some fruit and their findings. Ten of the spies reported that the land was dangerous and should be avoided:

So they brought to the people of Israel a bad report of the land that they had spied out, saying, "The land, through which we have gone to spy it out, is a land that devours its inhabitants, and all

> *the people that we saw in it are of great height . . . we seemed to ourselves like grasshoppers, and so we seemed to them.* (Numbers 13:32-33 ESV)

Two of the spies brought back a positive report filled with faith:

> *"Let us go up at once and occupy it, for we are well able to overcome it." (Numbers 13:30 ESV)*

Popular opinion won out and an entire generation missed out on the Land of Promise. I'd bet almost anything you can name the two spies with a positive report. If we were playing on *Jeopardy*, your answer would be, "Who are Joshua and Caleb?" And you'd be correct. Conversely, I'd bet everything I had, you can't name ONE of the ten spies with a negative report of warning and unbelief. Some of the names included "Shammua," "Palti" and "Gaddi." I'm not sure if any of you are looking for baby names? I'm guessing none of these made the list. But I know plenty of kids with the names Caleb and Joshua. These men had the courage to take a stand against the popular opinion of their day. God honored their courage to stand against the crowd, and they got to enter the Promised Land. In fact, God appointed Joshua to lead the people in:

> "<u>Be strong and courageous</u>, for you shall cause this people to inherit the land that I swore to their fathers to give them. Only <u>be strong and very courageous</u>, being careful to do according to all the law that Moses my servant commanded you. Do not turn from it to the right hand or to the left, that you may have good success wherever you go. This Book of the Law shall not depart from your mouth, but you shall meditate on it day and night, so that you may be careful to do according to all that is written in it. For then you will make your way prosperous, and then you will have good success. Have I not commanded you? <u>Be strong and courageous</u>. Do

not be frightened, and do not be dismayed, for the LORD your God is with you wherever you go." (Joshua 1:6-9 ESV)

BE STRONG AND COURAGEOUS

Some fears are funny. Did you know that Gustave Eiffel, the designer of the Eiffel Tower, was afraid of heights? Did you know that Walt Disney, the creator of Mickey Mouse, was afraid of mice? Did you know that Alexander the Great and Napoleon, who conquered much of the known world, were both afraid of cats! Not to be outdone, Genghis Khan was only afraid of two things, dogs and his mom! [2]

Some fears are funny and some fears are tragic. Fear is a thief. Don't let it rob you of your Promised Land. In order to possess the promises of God, you will need to "Be strong and courageous."

God doesn't just double down on courage. *Three* times He commands Joshua to be *"strong and courageous."* Pastor Rick Warren notes that the command to *"Fear not"* is one of the most repeated in the Bible. It occurs roughly 365 times [3], one for each day of the year! The pre-Christian philosopher Aristotle said, "Courage is the first virtue that makes all other virtues possible." I tend to agree with him. You might want to be generous. But if you're afraid of going broke, you won't be. You might want to be loving, but if you're afraid of putting yourself out there and getting hurt, you won't be. Courage is the primary virtue that makes all the other virtues possible. It is going to take courage to win in life.

Notice God said to *"be* strong and courageous," He didn't say to *"Feel* strong and courageous." That encourages me! I can feel afraid or anxious and still "be strong and courageous." Our nation's thirty-second president, Franklin D. Roosevelt, said, "Courage is not the absence of fear, but rather the assessment that something else is more important than fear." [4] For Joshua the applause of heaven meant more than the fear of man, and he led the people into the Promised Land.

Today, more than ever, you will feel an increase in pressure to agree with things you know to be false. Will you have the courage to take a stand? People need to see your courage. You may have seen the YouTube video that highlights the power of peer pressure. A hidden camera is placed on an elevator. All but one of the passengers are in on the "experiment." When people get onto the elevator, they intentionally face the wrong way until an unsuspecting girl gets on and faces the correct way. Each time the elevator stops and a new person gets on, they face the wrong way. Slowly, but surely the girl's confidence begins to erode. Each new person that enters and faces the wrong way chips away at her resolve until, finally, she caves in and faces the wrong way! The video is hilarious and sad all at once. [5]

Psychologist Solomon Asch conducted a similar experiment a number of times back in the 1950s. A series of three lines with varying lengths were drawn and labeled A, B, C. Afterwards another line was drawn that clearly matched the length of the line labeled C. Lines A and B were not even close.

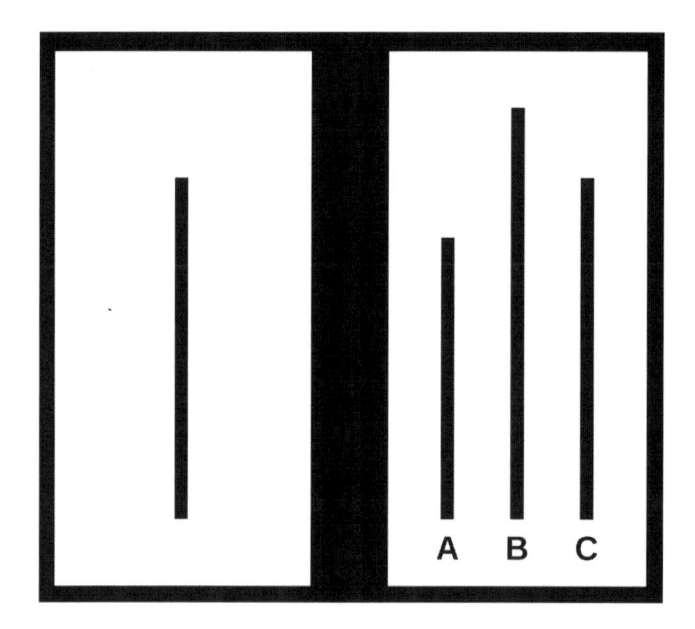

A room was set up to look like a classroom. All of the students were actors, except for one who became the unsuspecting subject of the experiment. When the professor asked the class which line matched the unlabeled line, the correct answer was obviously C. One by one, however, the class members answered A. When it came time for the unsuspecting student to answer, 35 percent of the time the student would deliberately give the wrong answer. Over a third of the times the experiment was conducted, the subject of the experiment would agree with something they knew to be false in order to fit in. After the experiment concluded, Asch commented, "That intelligent, well-meaning young people are willing to call white black is a matter of concern." [6]

There is good news though! The experiment continued with one small change. Someone else was added to the group that would give the right answer. When ONE person stepped up and gave the right answer, it gave the unsuspecting student the confidence to give the right answer as well. In fact, the number of people willing to go with the crowd dropped from 35 percent to just 5 percent.

One person willing to stand for what they knew to be true gave others the confidence to stand up for truth as well. It gave them courage! Remember the Trinity of guy movies? *Gladiator, Braveheart* and *300*. In *Braveheart*, William Wallace said it best, "Men don't follow titles, they follow courage." [7] The people followed Joshua right into the Promised Land. Will you be strong and courageous as you play the game of life?

THE SOURCE OF COURAGE

"Be strong and courageous. Do not be frightened, and do not be dismayed, for the LORD your God is with you wherever you go."
(Joshua 1:9 ESV)

The summer of 1996 changed everything for the Hartford Whalers hockey team. Up until this time, we lacked an identity. We lacked toughness. All that changed with the acquisition of six-foot, six-inch, 240-pound winger Stu Grimson. Stu was known around the league as "The Grim Reaper." He amassed over 2,000 penalty minutes in his NHL career. His presence alone struck fear into the opposition and gave us a newfound sense of courage. My motto was, "If Stu is for you, who can be against you!" In his letter to the Romans, the Apostle Paul will do us even one better. He says simply:

If God is for us, who can be against us? (Romans 8:31 ESV)

The presence of God brings courage. If God is for you, then who and what could ever stand against you?

In 2 Kings 18 and 19, Jerusalem is surrounded by the Assyrian army. The Assyrians were a brutal people specializing in torture and terror. They perfected the horrific art of skinning people alive for maximum suffering. They were known to impale their victims to serve as living "billboards" that read, "Don't mess with Assyria." King Hezekiah and the people of Jerusalem felt helpless and afraid as the Assyrian siege continued. But they weren't alone. King Hezekiah looked up and prayed to the Lord of Heaven. The Prophet Isaiah returned to the king with the word of the Lord:

"Therefore thus says the LORD concerning the king of Assyria: He shall not come into this city or shoot an arrow there, or come before it with a shield or cast up a siege mound against it. By the way that he came, by the same he shall return, and he shall not come into this city, declares the LORD. For I will defend this city to save it, for my own sake and for the sake of my servant David."
(2 Kings 19:32-34 ESV)

The following morning King Hezekiah awoke to find the dead bodies of 185,000 Assyrian soldiers outside the walls of Jerusalem. During the night, the Angel of the Lord fought on behalf of Hezekiah. *"If God be for you, who can be against you?"* The name Hezekiah literally means, "The Lord is my strength." Where do you find your strength? What's your source of courage?

SCARS TELL A STORY

In John 20 we hear the story of Jesus' conversation with his disciple, Thomas. "Doubting Thomas," as he's often referred to as, refused to believe the disciples report that Christ was risen from the dead. The only way he would believe was to touch the scars from Jesus' crucifixion on the cross. Jesus appeared to Thomas and invited him to feel His nail-pierced hands and wounded side:

> *"Put your finger here, and see my hands; and put out your hand, and place it in my side. Do not disbelieve, but believe."*
> *(John 20:27 ESV)*

I played fourteen years in the NHL, and I have the scars to prove it. Each scar has a story behind it. I have a decent scar over my left eye where I was gashed by a hockey stick during a game in Ottawa. I think the doctor used piano wire to sew me up. I took a slapshot to the face in North Bay. It broke my jaw in two places and left a scar on my chin. A constant reminder, I should have ducked. My back looks like a series of model railroad tracks after having five different back surgeries. Each surgery had a narrative behind it. Every scar tells a story.

Isn't it interesting that Jesus chose to keep His scars after His resurrection? His scars tell a story. His nail-pierced hands and feet are an eternal reminder of the tremendous price paid for our sin and God's unending love for you and me. His scars also tell another story. Did you know that scars on the body of a lion are evidence of its success. The more scars a lion has accrued over the years the more other animals see it as a fighter and a survivor. As a result, other animals stay out of its way. Jesus is the scarred Lion of the Tribe of Judah! He is battle tested. He is unrivaled and unequaled! He has grappled with death and won! He has defeated the Devil and all his demons! His scars are a sign and a signal to all who oppose Him. One day, every knee will bow and every tongue will confess that Jesus is Lord of all. The Lion is with you. His presence brings courage.

ENCOURAGE YOURSELF IN THE LORD

In 1 Samuel, we hear about the great King David at one of his lowest moments:

> *And David was greatly distressed: for the people spoke of stoning him, because the soul of all the people was grieved, every man for his sons, and for his daughters: but David encouraged himself in the LORD his God. (1 Samuel 30:6 WBT)*

I mean this in the kindest way possible: King David is better than you. Don't worry, he's better than me too. Some men pride themselves on their ability to hunt wild game. David killed a lion and a bear with his bare hands! See what I mean? He's better than you. Some men pride themselves on their ability to "throw hands" and fight. David beat up a nine-foot, nine-inch guy arrayed in battle armor. He's better than you. When David played the harp, demons would flee. Seriously, how do you make the harp that tough? How could he play it in such a way that all the demons in hell would flee? I couldn't tell you, but he did. He's better than you and me.

Even with all his gifts and successes, there came a moment in David's life when his world was coming undone. His village had just been plundered. All that he held dear was stolen from him. And now his men spoke of stoning him. Have you ever been there, in a place where all four walls of your life are caving in on top of you? As tough as he was, David found himself in trouble. What would he do? David learned to *"encourage himself in the Lord."* What do you do?

Winning the morning is how I encourage myself in the Lord. If I lose the morning, I usually lose the day, so every day I try to win. David learned to win the morning. In Psalm 108 he writes:

> *Awake, O harp and lyre! I will awake the dawn!*
> *(Psalm 108:2 ESV)*

David would begin his day with the praise and worship of God. Through music and song, he learned to win the morning and encouraged himself in the Lord. Mornings are critical to your success. Neuroscience tells us that the first twenty minutes of your morning will go a long way in shaping how you view the world. When you first wake up, your brain is still in what's known as the alpha state. In this state, your brain is like a "super highway" to your subconscious mind. You are literally framing the way you view the world. How devastating is it if the first thing you do is pump your brain full of Facebook, Instagram, and TikTok. David decided to fill his mind with thoughts of God first thing in the morning. In doing so, he encouraged himself in the Lord. He gave himself courage. By the way, David tracked down the marauders that raided his village. He received everything back again and then some. By winning the morning, he won the day. I want you to win.

GIVE EACH OTHER COURAGE

Encouragement and courage aren't things we should keep to ourselves. Just as we can encourage ourselves in the Lord, we can encourage each other. In fact, Hebrews teaches us to "stir" each other up with encouragement:

> *And let us consider how to stir up one another to love and good*
> *works, not neglecting to meet together, as is the habit of some,*
> *but encouraging one another, and all the more as you see the Day*
> *drawing near. (Hebrews 10:24-25 ESV)*

Muhammad Ali is without question the greatest boxer to ever live. He is an icon of the sport. But he didn't reach the pinnacle alone, he always had his corner man and friend beside him, Drew "Bundini" Brown. Bundini didn't just give Ali coaching, he gave him courage. Former Champ George Foreman, said of Bundini, "I wouldn't even call him a trainer or a corner man, he was more important than a trainer. Ali had unmeasurable determination and he got it from Bundini." [8] Among his other gifts, Bundini understood the power of words.

> ***Death and life are in the power of the tongue, and those who love it will eat its fruits. (Proverbs 18:21 ESV)***

If death and life are in the power of the tongue, then Bundini was definitely a "life-speaker." He spoke life into Ali's soul and courage into his heart. He taught him how to "float like a butterfly and sting like a bee." He declared things like, "You must be the prettiest," "You are the Greatest!" Ali did become the greatest, but not without the encouragement from his corner man and friend. At Bundini's funeral, Ali left a bouquet of flowers with a card that simply read, "YOU made me the Greatest." [9]

One of the greatest heroes of our faith is the Apostle Paul. Paul didn't get there alone. He had a "Bundini" of his own. His name was Joseph. In fact, Joseph was such an encourager, they gave him the nickname "Barnabas," which means "son of encouragement." Paul was going to need a lot of it. Here is just a snapshot of what Paul had to endure in his own words:

> *Five times I received at the hands of the Jews the forty lashes less one. Three times I was beaten with rods. Once I was stoned. Three times I was shipwrecked; a night and a day I was adrift at sea; on frequent journeys, in danger from rivers, danger from robbers, danger from my own people, danger from Gentiles, danger in the city, danger in the wilderness, danger at sea, danger from false brothers; in toil and hardship, through many a sleepless night, in*

hunger and thirst, often without food, in cold and exposure. And, apart from other things, there is the daily pressure on me of my anxiety for all the churches. (2 Corinthians 11:24-28 ESV)

If you ever think you're having a bad day, consider the life of Paul. You'll feel better. Through all of it, I can almost hear Barnabas giving Paul courage to keep going, "You float like a butterfly and sting like a bee!" OK, maybe he didn't say that, but I bet he reminded Paul, "You can do all things through Christ who strengthens you!" (Philippians 4:13). "Paul, greater is HE that is in you than he that is in the world!" (1 John 4:4) and "Paul, if God is for you, who can be against you!" (Romans 8:31). Paul went on to be the greatest missionary our faith has ever known. Do you have a Barnabas in your life? I know I do. You should BE a Barnabas, as well. Honestly, it's not that difficult to speak life and courage into another person. It's so easy a nine-year-old can do it.

Chris Davis of the Baltimore Orioles was in a hitting slump. In fact, this slump was historically bad. Davis batted fifty-four times without a hit. The Orioles were in Fenway Park to take on the Boston Red Sox. Davis was taking some extra batting practice as you might expect, when a nine-year-old boy named Henry Frasca gave a handwritten letter to the dugout security guard. The guard forwarded it to Chris. Here is what it said:

"Dear Mr Davis,

from Henry Frasca, a nine year old die hard Red Sox fan. There are 2 things I want you to know: First, the way you play baseball has nothing to do with how good a person you are. Also, you are incredible. You've played in the MLB. You've done it for a long time and everyone goes through a slump. Don't give up. We're rooting for you" [10]

Chris Davis, a bit choked up, folded up the letter and placed it in his Bible. That night Davis had three hits! The slump was over because a nine-year-old kid believed he could encourage and speak life into a grown man. We are changing young Henry's name to Barnabas. Who do you know that's in a slump? Who can you encourage today?

HEAVEN'S APPLAUSE

Therefore judge nothing before the appointed time; wait until the Lord comes. He will bring to light what is hidden in darkness and will expose the motives of the heart. At that time each will receive their praise from God. (1 Corinthians 4:5 NIV)

Ludwig van Beethoven was one of the greatest composers the world has ever known. His early success only made the pain of losing his hearing later in life that much worse. After all, who was he if he couldn't hear? In an effort to keep his lack of hearing a secret, Ludwig became a recluse. A deep depression started to set in. He not only lost his will to write music, he was losing his will to live. Almost as if by divine intervention, Beethoven received a newfound sense of hope. He realized he still had music inside of him to give to the world. He regained the will to live again and the will to write again.

Beethoven's final symphony was performed at Vienna's Theater am Kärntnertor on May 7, 1824. The aged and deaf composer insisted on conducting the symphony, despite the fact he couldn't hear. He would do this in tandem with the actual conductor who had led the musicians in practices, and could hear. Beethoven, with his back to the audience, faced the orchestra and began. He could feel the music reverberate throughout his body as each musician hit their notes. The beautiful harmony captivated the audience and for a little while, Ludwig forgot he was deaf. As the symphony ended, the elated crowd stood to their feet. "Bravo! Bravo!" they cheered without stopping. But Beethoven had no idea; his back was turned to the crowd the whole time and he couldn't hear the applause. Finally, the lead conductor took Beethoven by the arm and gently spun him around to face the audience. And there it was, a standing ovation and thunderous applause. [11]

I promise you, if you have the courage to live for God, if you choose to play for an audience of one, you will one day hear the praise of God and the applause of heaven. You may not hear it now, but one day you will. It will all be worth it. Christian courage is how you win in life. I want you to win.

CHAPTER 12

"MAKE YOUR LAST GAME YOUR BEST GAME" (TAKE YOUR SHOT)

In 2 Timothy, the Apostle Paul looks back on his life and says:

*I have fought the good fight, I have finished the race,
I have kept the faith. (2 Timothy 4:7 ESV)*

On December 28, 2000, the Atlanta Thrashers were about to face the New York Rangers at Madison Square Gardens. I had signed with Atlanta as a free agent in the off season, but I was not playing well. I was shuffled in and out of the lineup that season, and the coach told me I wouldn't play against the Rangers that evening. However, he did want me to take warmups in case someone got injured prior to the game, but that rarely happened.

I put on my gear, laced up my skates and took pregame warmups with my teammates at MSG. Afterwards, I had started taking my equipment off when Coach pulled me aside. "Adam, you're in! One of the guys was injured during warmups. Be ready to go!" Just like that, I was back in the game. We won convincingly that night 4–1. I logged a ton of ice time and played really well. In fact, Coach pulled me aside after the game and told me, "That's the best game I've ever seen you play." Little did I know it would be my last game. The following night we traveled to Long Island to take on the Islanders. I'd been experiencing some severe back pain, but just tried to muscle through it. My back held up for a whopping three minutes before several discs ruptured during the game. I would never play hockey again.

Early on in my NHL hockey career, it felt like playing hockey was never going to end. Then suddenly it did. Just like the eight and a half period marathon game against Pittsburgh (The Longest Game) felt like it was never going to end. But, suddenly, it did too. Our life may feel like it's never going to end. But, one day, it will. I pray on that day you hear the Lord tell you, "That's the best game I've ever seen you play." I hope your last game is your best game. James describes the brevity of life being like a vapor:

> *You do not know what will happen tomorrow.*
> *For what is your life? It is even a vapor that appears for a*
> *little time and then vanishes away. (James 4:14 NKJV)*

Greg Koehler's NHL career consisted of one shift totaling four seconds. The Carolina Hurricanes forward and Canadian native always dreamed of playing in the NHL. That dream was about to come to fruition on December 29, 2000. The Hurricanes were in Columbus to take on the Blue Jackets. Midway through the contest, Coach Paul Maurice called Greg's number and over the boards he went and skated into the action. His mother, watching the game on TV, screamed, "There he is!" And four seconds later, it was all over. Columbus took a penalty, the whistle blew, and Greg Koehler never played again. [1] He was never given another opportunity to play in that game or any other afterwards. Four seconds and it was over. When asked if he had any regrets about his NHL career, Koehler simply said "No, no regrets." He made the most of his four seconds. What will you do with your four seconds? Live each day as if it were your last. Because one day, it will be. Make your last game your best game.

"Our life is a vapor." In cosmic terms, it lasts four seconds and suddenly it's over. In Luke 12, Jesus tells us how NOT to use our four seconds. He tells the story of a self-absorbed rich man. This guy has an abundance of stuff. In fact, he has too much stuff. Rather than honoring God and being generous to people, he decided to hoard it all for himself. He built bigger barns to store his stuff and afterwards thinks, "Now, I can eat, drink, and be merry." Listen to God's response:

But God said to him, "Fool! This night your soul is required of you, and the things you have prepared, whose will they be?"
(Luke 12:20 ESV)

Translation: Your four seconds are up! You should have leveraged everything you had to love God and love people. Instead, YOU wasted your life focusing on the unholy Trinity: Me, Myself, and I. Now, your soul is required of you. Time is up.

What will you do with your four seconds? Abraham believed God and became the Father of Faith. Jacob wrestled with God and became Israel. Noah obeyed God and built an ark that rescued his family and, ultimately, the world. Solomon built the Temple and wrote the book of Proverbs. Isaiah spoke on behalf of God. Joshua made it clear what he was going to do with his four seconds:

"But as for me and my house, we will serve the LORD."
(Joshua 24:15 ESV)

What will you do with your four seconds? Make your last game your best game.

GO ALL IN

Cards played a powerful role in the childhood of Annie Duke. Her father was a professor and a workaholic. As a young girl, she always knew she could pull her dad away from his books if she brought out a deck of cards. He was wildly competitive and could not say no to a game. They didn't play kids games like Go Fish. They played mature games like Gin or Hearts. Pretty ambitious for a seven-year-old. Especially since her father would NEVER let her win.

Her mother, on the other hand, was a nonfunctioning alcoholic. She would spend her days sitting at the kitchen table with a cigarette and glass of scotch playing Solitaire. The only time young Annie ever felt in sync with her mom was when she pulled up a chair and played Solitaire alongside her.

Fast-forward about twenty years later, Annie graduated from Columbia and moved on to UPenn for her PhD. Driven and on a mission, she was killing it on all fronts, until the wheels fell off. The night before her dream internship, she had a panic attack and had to be hospitalized for a few weeks. As time passed, she still was unsure of what triggered her nervous breakdown and what to do next. Her older brother, a professional card player, suggested she join a local poker game. She walked into the dark, smoky room and sat at the card table. In that place, she felt strangely at home.

Annie's academic mind, coupled with her competitive spirit, made her uniquely suited for the world of poker. She excelled in the game and started creating a bit of a name for herself. In 2004, ESPN was broadcasting the "World Series of Poker: Tournament of Champions." They invited the top ten players from around the world to compete in a "Texas Hold 'Em" winner-take-all poker tournament. The grand prize was two million dollars. Annie was invited to compete. Some people speculate the reason she was invited to play was because she was a woman and ESPN thought it might be good for ratings. She knew how good she was, but she also wondered if she really belonged. [2]

The tournament began and Annie survived hand after hand as other players were eliminated. She made it down to the final three players! Ironically, one of her opponents was her brother. He was eliminated, and suddenly, Annie found herself playing head-to-head against Phil Hellmuth, the "Bad Boy of Poker." He was six feet, five inches tall and wore dark sunglasses. When he looked across the card table at you, it felt like he read your soul. He stared right through you.

The dealer distributes the cards. Annie has a "king, ten" in the hole. Hellmuth receives a "ten, eight." He opens the betting. She calls. He opens again and she calls again. He thinks she's bluffing. Another flop of the cards and suddenly, Annie goes ALL IN ! Now Hellmuth must decide, "Who has better cards?" [3]

That is the question you must answer if you're going to win in life. Who has better cards? Is it Jesus Christ and His Kingdom? Or is it the world and all it has to offer? The Prophet Elijah challenged God's people with the same question:

And Elijah came near to all the people and said, "How long will you go limping between two different opinions? If the LORD is God, follow him; but if Baal, then follow him." And the people did not answer him a word. (1 Kings 18:21 ESV)

Who has better cards? Jesus offers forgiveness of sins and eternal life. He offers peace that passes all understanding and unspeakable joy in his presence. That sounds like a great hand to be dealt. For the Christian, this life is as bad as it gets. For the non-Christian, this life is as good as it gets. Christians simply have better cards. And so did Annie Duke. She won the Tournament of Champions and the two million dollar grand prize. She went ALL IN because she believed she had better cards.

I want you to go ALL IN with Jesus. Please don't be the halfway guy or girl. Do you know what I mean? The type of person that is "kinda Christian"? You call yourself one, but don't actually live like one. You have a Bible, but never read it. You belong to a church, but never go to it. If being a Christian were a crime, would there be enough evidence to convict you? Don't be the halfway person. If you're going to live for Jesus, then live for Jesus! If you'd rather just embrace sin and all the "world" has to offer, then just do that. The halfway person loses on all fronts. That person has too much God to enjoy sin and too much of the world to make a difference. That person gets the worst of both worlds. Being a halfway Christian is attractive to no one, least of all Jesus. In fact, Jesus warns the church at Laodicea against being halfway or "lukewarm":

> *"I know your works: you are neither cold nor hot. Would that you were either cold or hot! So, because you are lukewarm, and neither hot nor cold, I will spit you out of my mouth."*
> *(Revelation 3:15-16 ESV)*

Nobody wants lukewarm coffee, lukewarm food or lukewarm Christians. Go ALL IN for God. He is on the lookout for ALL IN people:

> *"The eyes of the LORD search the whole earth in order to strengthen those whose hearts are fully committed to him."*
> *(2 Chronicles 16:9 NIV)*

PLAY YOUR PART IN GOD'S STORY

The psalmist in Psalm 139 talks about our place in God's story:

Your eyes saw my unformed substance; in your book were written, every one of them, the days that were formed for me, when as yet there was none of them. (Psalm 139:16 ESV)

I failed to mention that I'm somewhat of a movie star. No, I didn't receive an Oscar or anything like that, but I played my part well. The movie was the 1992 critically acclaimed film *The Mighty Ducks*. [4] Hey, man, don't judge me! I was in the movie even though I didn't know it then. At the time, I was playing for the Hartford Whalers. We were in Minnesota to take on the Stars. It was just another game for us. Later, we discovered that Disney was there to film a few scenes for their upcoming movie. It was no longer just another game. I had a great game—two goals and an assist! For a guy who only had thirty-seven goals during his entire career, a two-goal game was massive. I was sure Disney would show me scoring one of my goals or maybe even both of them! But no. Nothing! Absolutely nothing! Not me scoring. Not me skating or hitting someone. Nothing! I'm in the film though. If you slow the video way down, you can see me sitting on the bench, and I think in another scene, my left arm makes it in the shot. It wasn't much, but I was in the movie. I played my part in the story. God has a part for you in His story.

> *For we are his workmanship, created in Christ Jesus*
> *for good works, which God prepared beforehand,*
> *that we should walk in them. (Ephesians 2:10 ESV)*

God has a role for you to play in His epic story of life. He has "good works" for you to "walk in." Whether your part is big or small, play it well. Be the best you can be for the glory of God and the good of people. Play your part.

TAKE YOUR SHOT

You miss 100 percent of the shots you don't take.
—*Wayne Gretzky* [6]

Don't believe everything you see in the movies. *The Mighty Ducks* film made it look like we lost to Minnesota 4–3. It's not true. We actually tied the game 3–3 and went into overtime. With two seconds remaining in the overtime, I scored and we won. Only two seconds left. It seemed like so little time, but it was all that I needed to take my shot. There is still time on the clock for you. Take your shot!

- David took his shot and defeated Goliath.
- Moses took his shot and delivered God's people out of slavery.
- Twelve "nobodies" decided to take their shot and follow Jesus. They became the Twelve Disciples that God used to change the world.
- A thief hanging next to Jesus on the cross had only seconds left: He took his shot and asked, "Jesus, remember me when you enter into your Kingdom." Two seconds was enough for Jesus to respond, "Today, you will be with me in paradise." He took his shot and scored an eternal reward.

I want you to win, and so does Jesus. I hope you take your shot, while there is still time on the clock. Hurry, He's coming soon:

"Behold, I am coming soon, bringing my recompense with me, to repay each one for what he has done. I am the Alpha and the Omega, the first and the last, the beginning and the end."
(Revelation 22:12-13 ESV)

ENDNOTES

SECTION 1 "MISSING THE MARK"

[1] "Off-target at Olympics, Matt Emmons No Stranger to Adversity, *USA Today*, https://www.usatoday.com/story/sports/olympics/2016/07/08/emmons-no-stranger-to-adversity/86879070/.

[2] Family Feud, "DUMBEST ANSWERS EVER! Steve Harvey is SPEECHLESS!" YouTube Video, November 5, 2019, YouTube, https://youtu.be/HeGVeBWECu8.

[3] Lewis, C. S., *Mere Christianity*, 1952, <a href="https://kwize.com/C.-S.-Lewis-quotes">C. S. Lewis</a>, Mere Christianity (1952).

CHAPTER 1

[1] Spain, S., "Runs in the Family," Espn.com. https://www.espn.com/espn/feature/story/_/id/24505521/the-jaw-dropping-story-nfl-coach-search-family#:~:text=It%20was%20about%20a%20life,I%20started%20thinking%20about%20Deland.%22.

[2] "Identity Theft,"West Long Branch Police Department, West Long Branch, New Jersey, https://www.westlongbranch.org/police-department/pages/identity-theft#:~:text=The%20FTC%20estimates%20that%20as,until%20it%20is%20too%20late.

CHAPTER 2

[1] "David Ayres," Wikipedia, accessed July 29, 2024, https://en.m.wikipedia.org/wiki/David_Ayres.

[2] Truss, D., "The Opposite of Depression," Daily-Ink by David Truss, https://daily-ink.davidtruss.com/the-opposite-of-depression/.

[3] Briggs, M., "God Used Rick Warren's 'The Purpose Driven Life' to Rescue Michael Phelps From Suicide," Churchleaders.com, August 8, 2020, https://churchleaders.com/daily-buzz/284468-michael-phelps-suicide-purpose-driven-life.html.

[4] "Pastor Matt Chandler: These Are the Days God Has Designed for Me," Movieguide.org, accessed May 10, 2024, https://www.movieguide.org/news-articles/matt-chandler-these-are-the-days-god-has-designed-for-me.html#:~:text=%E2%80%9CPsalm%20139%20ends%20it%20with,really%20am%20one%20of%20one.

[5] Minkoff, Rob and Roger Allers, dir, *The Lion King*, United States: Walt Disney Studios, 1994.

CHAPTER 3

[1] "Adam Burt", Hockeyfights.com, https://www.hockeyfights.com/players/326.

[2] Poss, J., "What's Wrong, Chesterton?" February 28, 2019, Jordanmposs.com, https://www.jordanmposs.com/blog/2019/2/27/whats-wrong-chesterton.

[3] "List of Highest-grossing Superhero Films," Wikipedia, accessed September 7,2024, https://en.m.wikipedia.org/wiki/List_of_highest-grossing_superhero_films#:~:text=Highest%2Dgrossing%20superhero%20film%20franchises%20and%20series,-See%20also%3A%20List&text=The%20Marvel%20Cinematic%20Universe%20ranks,nearly%20%241.9%20billion%20per%20film.

CHAPTER 4

[1] "Michael A. Monsoor," Wikipedia, accessed August 24, 2024, https://en.m.wikipedia.org/wiki/Michael_A._Monsoor.

[2] "Michael A. Monsoor, 25," *Los Angeles Times,* https://projects.latimes.com/wardead/name/michael-a-monsoor/.

[3] Weyandt, J., "One Dad to Another: Father Restoring Car That Is Link to Man's Beloved Son, *The Tennessean,* June 15, 2014, https://www.tennessean.com/story/news/2014/06/15/one-dad-another-father-restoring-car-link-mans-beloved-son/10545841/.

[4] Harris, R., "Our Longing for Our Heavenly Home," *The Gospel Coalition*, February 3, 2021, https://au.thegospelcoalition.org/article/our-longing-for-our-heavenly-home/?amp=1.

[5] Keller, T, "Everything Bad Is Going to Come Untrue," *Christianity Today,* https://www.christianitytoday.com/2023/08/tim-keller-september-11-sermon-everything-bad-come-untrue/.

[6] Smith, B., "Old Man and a Bucket of Shrimp," Rotary E-Club of Houston, https://www.rotaryclubhouston.org/stories/old-man-and-a-bucket-of-shrimp#:~:text=Eddie%20Rickenbacker%20lived%20many%20years,a%20heart%20full%20of%20gratitude.

[7] Elias, R., "Ric Elias: 3 Things I Learned While My Plane Crashed, Lingq.com, https://www.lingq.com/en/learn-english-online/courses/88164/ric-elias-3-things-i-learned-while-my-239284/.

SECTION 2 'TRAINING TO WIN"
[1] O'Connor, Gavin, dir, Miracle, United States: Walt Disney Pictures, 2004.

CHAPTER 5
[1] Levenson, E., "This Home on Mexico Beach Survived Hurricane Michael. That's No Coincidence," CNN.com, October 16, 2018, https://www.cnn.com/2018/10/15/us/mexico-beach-house-hurricane-trnd/index.html.

[2] Maher, B., Goodreads.com, https://www.goodreads.com/quotes/944012-to-most-christians-the-bible-is-like-a-software-license.

[3] Mauro, Philip, "Life in the Word," in *The Fundamentals: A Testimony to the Truth* (Los Angeles: Bible Institute of Los Angeles, 1917), 144–208.

[4] Bloom, L. A. C., "Want More And Better Sex? Get Married And Stay Married," Huffpost.com, July 13, 2017, https://www.huffpost.com/entry/want-more-and-better-sex-get-married-and-stay-married_b_5967b618e4b022b-b9372aff2.

[5] Emba, C., "Consent Is Not Enough. We Need a New Sexual Ethic," Washingtonpost.com, March 17, 2022, https://www.washingtonpost.com/opinions/2022/03/17/sex-ethics-rethinking-consent-culture/.

[6] Ortberg, J. "John Ortberg," Goodreads.com, https://www.goodreads.com/quotes/647332-christianity-is-like-a-nail-he-yemelian-yaroslavsky-the-harder

[7] Bruner, R., "The Bible: The Best Loved and Most Hated Book on the Earth," Livingaschristians.com, February 9, 2020, https://www.livingaschristians.com/resources/2020/02/09/the-bible-the-best-loved-and-most-hated-book-on-the-earth.

[8] Spurgeon, C., "Charles Spurgeon Quotes," February 9, 2020, Azquotes.com, Charles Spurgeon Quotes.

[9] Saint Augustine, *Confessiones* (Milan: Johannes Bonus, 21 July 1475).

[10] Gear, S. D., "Did St Augustine Say This to a Prostitute?" Truthchallenge.one. https://www.truthchallenge.one/blog/2014/11/17/did-st-augustine-say-this-to-a-prostitute/.

CHAPTER 6

[1] Keenan, M., "Why Couples Really Divorce: Top 10 Reasons For Divorce (UK)," Divorce-Online.co.uk., accessed April 27, 2024, https://www.divorce-online.co.uk/blog/reasons-for-divorce/.

[2] Zouves, N., "Second Chances: 'I survived jumping off the Golden Gate Bridge,'" *ABC News,* May 18,2017, Abc7news.com. https://abc7news.com/golden-gate-bridge-suicides-suicide-survivors-jump-survive/201.

[3] Raguz, N., "When Stacey King joked about his contributions on Michael Jordan's career-high scoring night," Si.com, accessed November 11, 2023, https://www.si.com/nba/bulls/old-school/when-stacey-king-joked-about-his-contributions-on-michael-jordans-career-high-scoring-night#:~:text=%22I'll%20always%20remember%20this,and%20Cavs%2C%20117%2D113.

[4] Shadyak, Tom, dir, *Bruce Almighty,* United States: Spyglass Entertainment, 2003.

[5] Batterson, M., CHASE THE LION: If Your Dream Doesn't Scare You, It's Too Small (New York: Multnomah), 44.

[6] Keller, T., "Tim Keller," Goodreads.com. https://www.goodreads.com/quotes/338379-god-will-only-give-you-what-you-would-have-asked.

CHAPTER 7

[1] Brener, J., "NineteenYears Ago: Maurice Cheeks Assists National Anthem Singer," Blazersedge.com, April 25, 2022, https://www.blazersedge.com/2022/4/25/23041209/portland-trail-blazers-history-nba-maurice-cheeks-assists-national-anthem-singer.

[2] "Lessons from the Dungys," Indval.org. http://www.indval.org/Articles/Article27.htm.

[3] Warren, R, "Living on Purpose with Rick Warren—The Purpose Driven Life," The Aggressive Life, February 6, 2024, https://podcasts.apple.com/us/podcast/the-aggressive-life-with-brian-tome/id1472047907?i=1000644330667.

CHAPTER 8

[1] Jacquez, J., "The Story Behind the St. Louis Blues's Victory Song 'Gloria,'" News-Leader.com, June 13, 2019, https://www.news-leader.com/story/sports/2019/06/13/st-louis-blues-gloria-song-laura-branigan-stanley-cup-hockey-nhl/1451175001/.

[2] Clair, M., "How the Pirates Chose 'We Are Family' in '79," Mlb.com, February 19, 2022, https://www.mlb.com/news/how-the-pirates-chose-we-are-family-as-their-anthem.

[3] Parris, M., "As an Atheist, I Truly Believe Africa Needs God," Thetimes.com, December 27, 2008, https://www.thetimes.com/article/as-an-atheist-i-truly-believe-africa-needs-god-3xj9bm80h8m.

[4] Atlas, D., "Residents of Possum Trot, Texas, Adopt 76 Foster Children," People.com, August 30, 2012, https://people.com/human-interest/texas-town-residents-adopt-76-foster-children/.

[5] "Sound of Hope: The Story of Possum Trot," Wikipedia, September 5, 2024, https://en.m.wikipedia.org/w/index.php?title=Sound_of_Hope:_The_Story_of_Possum_Trot&action=history.

[6] Jason Schlosberg, "Battle at Kruger," YouTube video, May 3, 2007, https://m.youtube.com/watch?v=LU8DDYz68kM.

[7] Ross, Gary, dir., *Seabiscuit*, United States: Universal Pictures, 2003.

[8] "African Proverb – Cooperation," Teachdifferent.com. https://teachdifferent.com/podcast/if-you-want-to-go-fast-go-alone-if-you-want-to-go-far-go-together-teach-different-with-an-african-proverb-cooperation/.

[9] "Slogans of the United States Army," Wikipedia, accessed August 6, 2024, https://en.m.wikipedia.org/w/index.php?title=Slogans_of_the_United_States_Army&action=history.

[10] Brettscneider, M., "Redwoods, Roots, and the Power of Connection," Damselwings.com, October 6, 2018, https://damselwings.com/2018/10/06/redwoods-roots-power-of-connection/#:~:text=Coastal%20redwoods'%20root%20systems%2C%20though,other%20redwoods%20for%20added%20stability.

[11] Scott, Ridley, dir, *Gladiator*, United States: Dreamworks Pictures, 2000.

[12] Obu, R. N., "Going to Church Prolongs YourLlife by Fourteen Years," Myjoyonline.com, October 11, 2023, https://www.myjoyonline.com/going-to-church-prolongs-your-life-by-14-years/.

[13] "GOING TO CHURCH OFTEN IS GOOD FOR YOUR MENTAL HEALTH," Undeceptions.com. https://undeceptions.com/articles/going-to-church-is-good-for-your-mental-health/#:~:text=%E2%80%9C(Furthermore)%-2520those%2520who%2520attend,phenomenon%2520observed%2520in%2520the%2520US.

[14] Stanton, G., "Does Faith Reduce Divorce Risk?" Thepublicdiscourse.com, March 22, 2018, https://www.thepublicdiscourse.com/2018/03/20935/#:~:-

text=Most%20recently%2C%20research%20conducted%20at,by%20a%20 remarkable%2047%20percent.

[15] Vanderweele, T. J., & Case, B., "Empty Pews Are an American Public Health Crisis," Christianitytoday.com, November 22, 2021, www.christianity-today.com/2021/10/church-empty-pews-are-american-public-health-crisis/.

[16] Ibid.

SECTION 3 "PLAYING TO WIN"

[1] Algar, S., "Mets Crasher Rafael Diaz Out of Jail, Says He 'Got Caught Up in the Moment'," Nypost.com, June 4, 2012, https://nypost.com/2012/06/04/mets-crasher-rafael-diaz-out-of-jail-says-he-got-caught-up-in-the-moment/.

[2] Griffiths, E., "Eleven Stars Who Turned Down Major Movie Roles—and Who They Were Replaced by," Hellomagazine.com, accessed August 30, 2024, https://www.hellomagazine.com/film/715588/stars-who-turned-down-iconic-movie-roles/.

CHAPTER 9

[1] St. Augustine, Quotefancy.com, accessed August 30, 2024, https://quotefancy.com/quote/905805/Saint-Augustine-Love-God-and-do-whatever-you-please-for-the-soul-trained-in-love-to-God.

[2] "Who Are You Carrying the Stone For?" Journey Through Life, April 10, 2014, https://ty2008.wordpress.com/2014/04/10/who-are-you-carrying-the-stone-for/.

[3] Walleik, G., "MLB Legend Rod Carew And The Former NFL Pro Who Gave Him A New Heart," Only A Game, September 28, 2018, https://www.wbur.org/onlyagame/2018/09/28/rod-carew-konrad-reuland-heart-assists.

[4] Ong, G., "I Wanted to Tell my Dad How Much I Hated Him," Only A Game, April 1, 2019, https://www.wbur.org/onlyagame/2018/09/28/rod-carew-konrad-reuland-heart-assists.

[5] "Towel Power," Wikipedia, accessed August 23, 2024, https://en.m.wikipedia.org/wiki/Towel_Power.

[6] Ortberg, J. (2012). J., Who Is This Man? THE UNPREDICTABLE IMPACT OF THE INESCAPABLE JESUS (Zondervan, 2012), 38–43.

CHAPTER 10

[1] "Babe Ruth," Wikipedia, accessed September 7, 2024, https://en.m.wikipedia.org/wiki/Babe_Ruth.

[2] "Babe Ruth," Goodreads.com, https://www.goodreads.com/quotes/328460-never-let-the-fear-of-striking-out-keep-you-from.

[3] "Ty Cobb," Wikipedia, accessed August 25, 2024, https://en.m.wikipedia.org/wiki/Ty_Cobb.

[4] "Michael Jordan," Brainyquote.com, https://www.brainyquote.com/quotes/michael_jordan_127660.

[5] DiNuzzo, E., "Sixteen Famous 'Failures' of Wildly Successful People," *Reader's Digest,* July 17, 2024, https://www.rd.com/list/ironic-failures-of-wildly-successful-people/.

[6] "James J. Corbett," Wikipedia, accessed August 13, 2024, https://en.m.wikipedia.org/wiki/James_J._Corbett.

[7] "James Corbett," Goodreads.com, https://www.goodreads.com/quotes/540142-fight-one-more-round-when-your-feet-are-so-tired.

[8] Wiersbe, W. W., Quotefancy.com, https://quotefancy.com/quote/931741/Warren-W-Wiersbe-Most-Christians-are-being-crucified-on-a-cross-between-two-thieves.

[9] Cimini, R., "Jets Bury Ball, Put Patriots Game to Bed," Espn.com, December 8, 2010, https://www.espn.com/new-york/nfl/news/story?id=5899769.

[10] Batterson, M., *WIN THE DAY: 7 Daily Habits to Help You Stress Less and Accomplish More,* (New York: Multnomah, 2020), 38.

[11] "The Question of God," Pbs.org, https://www.pbs.org/wgbh/questionofgod/ownwords/mere2.html#:~:text=From%20Mere%20Christianity%20(1952)%20book,Forgiveness.

[12] Smedes, Lewis B., Brainyquotes.org, https://www.brainyquote.com/quotes/lewis_b_smedes_135524

[13] Boom, C. T., "Corrie Ten Boom: Forgiveness and a Bell Rope," in Regeneration, Repentance and Reformation, January 2, 2014, https://regenerationandrepentance.wordpress.com/2014/01/02/corrie-ten-boom-forgiveness-and-a-bell-rope/.

[14] "The Creation of Adam," Wikipedia accessed August 27, 2024 https://en.m.wikipedia.org/wiki/The_Creation_of_Adam.

[15] "Apathy in Churches Looms Large for Pastors," Lifeway Research, https://research.lifeway.com/2022/05/10/apathy-in-churches-looms-large-for-pastors/#:~:text=In%20the%20final%20release%20from,church%20and%20in%20their%20community.%E2%80%9D

[16] "Little Roosevelt and the Zeal," Theodore Roosevelt Center, https://www.theodorerooseveltcenter.org/Research/Digital-Library/Record/ImageViewer?libID=o288665.

[17] Klein, C., "When Teddy Roosevelt Was Shot in 1912, a Speech May Have Saved His Life," History.com. accessed July 15, 2024, https://www.history.com/news/shot-in-the-chest-100-years-ago-teddy-roosevelt-kept-on-talking.

[18] Tennant, Andy, dir, *Hitch*, United States: Columbia Pictures, 2005.

[19] "What Do Van Halen & Brown M&M's Have To Do With Safety?" Safety Dimensions. https://www.safetydimensions.com.au/van-halen/.

[20] "Checkmate Painting," Chesslovin.com, https://chesslovin.com/checkmate-painting/.

CHAPTER 11

[1] "Mark Brunell," Wikipedia, accessed August 26, 2024, https://en.m.wikipedia.org/wiki/Mark_Brunell.

[2] "List of Phobias A to Z," Fearaz.com, https://fearaz.com/171-bizarre-phobias-of-famous-people/.

[3] Weber, C., "Rick Warren: Why God Encourages Christians to 'Fear Not' 365 Times in the Bible," *The Christian Post*, April 30, 2016, https://www.christianpost.com/news/rick-warren-why-god-encourages-christians-to-fear-not-365-times-in-the-bible.html.

[4] "Franklin Roosevelt," Goodreads.com, https://www.goodreads.com/quotes/172689-courage-is-not-the-absence-of-fear-but-rather-the.

[5] Geviide25, "WYFFT: Would You Fall For That – Elevator," YouTube Video, January 30, 2015, http://www.Youtube.com/@Geviide2579, https://m.youtube.com/watch?v=dDAbdMv14Is.

[6] "Asch Conformity Experiments," Wikipedia, accessed May 12, 2024, https://en.m.wikipedia.org/wiki/Asch_conformity_experiments.

[7] Gibson, Mel, dir, *Braveheart*, United States: Paramount, 1995.

[8] Ping, D, "Bundini Brown: The Source of Muhammad Ali's Spirit," Thebokey.com., March 21, 2020, https://thebokey.com/2020/03/21/bundini-brown-the-source-of-muhammad-alis-spirit/.

[9] Frommer, F. J., "'You Made Me the Greatest': Muhammad Ali's Beloved Cornerman was Jewish," Forward.com, February 16, 2023, https://forward.com/news/sports/536529/muhammad-ali-jewish-drew-bundini-brown-cornerman-float-like-butterfly/.

[10] Murphy, H., "Boy Meets Orioles Player After Sending Him Supportive Letter: 'Everyone Goes Through a Slump,'" People.com, August 27, 2019, https://people.com/sports/boy-meets-orioles-player-after-sending-letter/.

[11] "Beethoven's Symphony No. 9 Debuts," History.com, https://www.history.com/this-day-in-history/beethoven-ninth-symphony-debuts-vienna#.

CHAPTER 12

[1] Baugh, P., "Greg Koehler's NHL Career Consisted of One Shift Totaling Four Seconds. Nytimes.com. November 8, 2023, https://www.nytimes.com/athletic/5037544/2023/11/08/nhl-4-second-shift-greg-koehler/.

[2] Duke, A., "A House Divided. Player," Themoth.org., July 20, 2011, https://player.themoth.org/#/?actionType=ADD_AND_PLAY&storyId=971.

[3] Duke, A., "I Won $2 Million At A Poker Tournament No One Thought I Deserved To Be At," Huffingtonpost.co.uk. June 9, 2019, https://www.huffingtonpost.co.uk/entry/annie-duke-poker_uk_5d7210d5e4b06d55b97183e3.

[4] Herek, Stephen, dir, *Mighty Ducks*, United States: Walt Disney Pictures, 1992.

[5] Gretzky, W., Brainyquotes.com, https://www.brainyquote.com/search_results?q=Wayne+Gretzky+.